WORLD'S GREATEST ARCHITECT

WORLD'S GREATEST ARCHITECT

Making, Meaning, and Network Culture

WILLIAM J. MITCHELL

The MIT Press
Cambridge, Massachusetts
London, England

For information on quantity discounts, email special_sales@mitpress.mit.edu.

This book was set in Scala and Scala Sans by The MIT Press.
Printed and bound in the United States of America.

Library of Congress Cataloging-in-Publication Data

Mitchell, William J. (William John), 1944–.
World's greatest architect : making, meaning, and network culture / William J. Mitchell.
p. cm.
Includes index.
ISBN 978-0-262-63364-2 (pbk. : alk. paper)
1. Architecture and society—History—21st century. 2. Cities and towns. I. Title.
NA2543.S6M57 2008
724'.7—dc22 2008000646

10 9 8 7 6 5 4 3 2 1

CONTENTS

PROLOGUE: MAKING MEANING

For millions of years—ever since our distant ancestors began to fashion simple stone tools—human beings have, simultaneously, been makers of things and makers of meaning.

We are programmed to extract meaning from just about everything. I'm no sociobiologist, but I am convinced by abundant evidence that this is part of our genetic endowment—a capability derived from evolutionary advantage. It is not hard to imagine that the cavemen who survived and reproduced were the ones who could most accurately read the opportunities and threats offered by terrain, weather, and other living creatures.

It was a short step from reading nature—which is utterly indifferent to human needs and purposes—to reading artifacts. And artifacts do have *intentions* behind them. They are made by particular individuals and groups *for* particular purposes, and they often communicate those purposes. Someone might shape a stone to serve as a weapon, and then pick it up to convey a threat—one that is not hard to understand.

In general, then, the artifacts that people produce, circulate, and use play dual roles in daily life. They both serve physical purposes and carry messages from their makers. We are adept at reading these messages, and the information that we receive in this way guides our actions.

Furthermore, artifacts do not act in isolation. The physical functions of elementary artifacts can be composed to form systems of interrelated parts such as machines, while their meanings can be composed to form more complex expressions such as pictures and works of architecture. For example: mechanical engineers compose mechanisms to produce needed motions; structural engineers compose members to produce frames that transfer loads to the ground; figurative sculptors compose pieces of shaped metal to represent kings and generals; and flower arrangers compose cut blossoms in water-filled vases, according to established conventions, to decorate rooms. The world of artifacts is organized into hierarchies of elements, subsystems, and systems—all of which both serve utilitarian purposes and signify.

From a narrowly focused engineer's perspective, physical functionality is what's important; selecting, shaping, and composing elements and subsystems to produce useful systems is the intellectually engaging game; and the messages carried (perhaps inadvertently) by these compositions are a relatively incidental matter of "aesthetics." It doesn't much matter to the engineer whether a column is Doric, Ionic, Corinthian, or Corbusian so long as it supports the roof.

From a cultural anthropologist's viewpoint, though, physical functionality fades into the background. The roles of artifacts as signs, symbols, and emblems, components of more extended and elaborate symbolic constructions, and transmitters of culture become crucial. Anthropologists, architectural historians, and cultural critics recognize that the need to hold up the roof does not fully determine a column's form—many combinations of material and section modulus would suffice, so the significance of the designer's particular choice of form and materials is what engages their interest.

The most commonplace messages carried by artifacts are announcements, by virtue of resemblance to other things whose functions we know, of what they are for: "This is a handle for opening the door."

Without these sorts of announcements, we would not know what to do with the things we encountered, and we would hardly be able to function ourselves. When door handles are broad and flat, for instance, they announce that they are for pushing, and when they are shaped for comfortable grasping they announce that they are for pulling. When designers choose handle shapes that are ambiguous, or—worse—that send messages that are inconsistent with the way the door actually swings, they create confusion.

To make sure that their announcements of intended use get through, designers often rhetorically heighten them. Thus push bars on doors may be broader and flatter than they really need to be to accommodate the user's palm, while handles for pulling may exaggerate their fit to the contours of grasping and pulling fingers.

Where elements play visible roles in larger systems, designers frequently employ similar rhetoric to show us how these systems work. In a pin-jointed roof truss, for instance, some members will be in tension and others will be in compression. The structural roles of these members become clear, and the way they work together to form a functioning truss becomes legible, if the designer makes the tension members dramatically thinner and the tension members visibly thicker. This principle is carried to a vivid extreme in tensegrity structures, where tension members reduce to wires and compression members become rigid rods.

Designers may also try to convey positive associations, and hence generate desire to acquire and use or inhabit their products, through the devices of metonymy and synecdoche. They often employ natural materials—Carrara marble, Norwegian wood, rich Corinthian leather, and so on—both to provide necessary functionality and to evoke highly regarded places of origin. On college campuses, architects may reuse recognizably classical or medieval architectural elements—either actual relics or modern fakes—to suggest connections to canonical past eras and the continuity of tradition. And product designers are often required to adhere closely to the brand image guidelines of "trusted" corporations—

which is why BMWs are instantly recognizable as BMWs, and Prada bags (real or fake) as Prada bags.

Finally, to conclude this brief and far from exhaustive catalogue, designers may deploy emblems and visual metaphors to refer and allude to other things. Within the language of classical architecture, to take a well-known example, designers can choose from a well-defined lexicon of Tuscan, Doric, Ionic, Corinthian, and Composite columns. Tuscan and Doric are sturdy, while Ionic, Corinthian, and Composite are increasingly slim and elegant. To those who are versed in this language, the thicker, stronger columns carry allusions of masculinity, while the daintier columns are feminine. Even more specifically, by tradition, each column type refers to particular gods and goddesses in the Greek and Roman pantheons. Furthermore, capitals sculpturally represent things—volutes, acanthus leaves, sometimes flowers—that have mythic significance. Selection from among the alternatives, then, is largely governed by considerations of decorum—of producing evocations that are appropriate to a building's context and use. The classical orders might seem lost in the dusty past, but the iconography of, say, fashionable sneakers—in masculine and feminine versions, with carefully constructed references to sports heroes, and powerful conventions of cool and uncool usage—isn't so different.

Not surprisingly, the dual service of artifacts as functional objects and as carriers of messages continually generates difficulties for designers, who have to keep the requirements of both roles in mind. A column may need to be beefed up in order to support the roof, but the rules of the Corinthian order may require it to be slimmer. A sneaker shape may be functional but no longer in style. The old slogan "form follows function" may express a sometime aspiration, but in practice the requirements for efficient functioning and effective communication of a message in a given context are not necessarily the same. Even worse, the syntax that guides composition of physical functions does not necessarily match the syntax structuring composition of meanings. So designers struggle to find ways of reconciling the two, often-conflicting sets of demands.

Even when they succeed in this, their victories may only be temporary, since the functions and meanings they intend may not be the functions and meanings that are subsequently assigned by users. A flat, rectangular wooden slab intended to serve as a door might, for example, be repurposed by some user as a tabletop—one that is emblematic of a casual, bohemian lifestyle. An innocent two-by-four, designed to serve as a structural member, might be picked up and used as a weapon. As Marcel Duchamp realized, a toilet fixture might be removed from its usual context, declared a "fountain," and exhibited in an art gallery. Any relationship that a designer establishes between function and meaning is therefore unstable. Often, as a result, artifacts announce their previous or alternative functions rather than their current ones. Or, under critical reading, they may disclose ironies, tensions, and contradictions in their messages that their originators had been unaware of.

Furthermore, material signifiers, unlike spoken words cannot be chosen freely from a mental stock. They are subject to the exigencies of supply chains, making some of them common and inexpensive in any given context, and others rare and costly; you might want a finely crafted table of solid wood to lend dignity to your dining room, but you might have to settle for a plywood door on trestles from Home Depot.

In the world of physical artifacts, then, functions and meanings are entangled in varied and complex ways. Sometimes designed objects primarily play physical roles, in which case we tend to think of them as engineering components or subsystems. Sometimes they serve mostly to communicate, in which case we tend to think of them as advertisements, fashion statements, art objects, or decoration. Most often, they are complex blends of physical functionality and significance, in which the designer has chosen some tradeoff point between satisfying the requirements of one versus satisfying those of the other.

To reduce the need for making difficult tradeoffs, it helps to have some way of separating physical and symbolic tasks. In other words, we need systems of *abstract*, dematerialized, cost-free artifacts that can serve, in efficiently specialized ways, almost entirely as carriers of messages.

This articulation of tasks resembles the modernist architectural strategy of separating the structural and weatherproofing roles of traditional masonry walls. Load-bearing columns provide structure, while a glass curtain wall provides weatherproofing. The columns can then be optimized for their more specialized, structural purpose, while the curtain walls can serve solely as a transparent, waterproof membranes—allowing them to become vanishingly light and thin.

Robert Venturi's well-known polemical distinction between a restaurant in the form of a duck and one treated as a decorated shed illustrates the point even more clearly. In the ducklike building, the outer shell must serve both as enclosure and as a sign advertising what is to be found inside—Long Island duckling. But it isn't so easy to jam restaurant seating and a kitchen into a supersized duck, not to mention that ducks don't have doors, windows, or loading docks. In the decorated shed, by contrast, the functions of the enclosure and the sign out front are separated, so that each can have the form and materials appropriate to its role. The shed can be shaped pragmatically, in response to the internal space needs. It doesn't have to *say* much. The sign—perhaps showing a painted duck—can be large but inexpensively constructed, prominently located, and vivid. Apart from conveying information, it doesn't have to *do* much.

Spoken language first met the need for a separate, extremely lightweight system of artifacts optimized for communication. You can think of spoken words as transient signs out in front of your face. They enable you, for instance, to shout a threat instead of picking up a stick. They certainly aren't entirely ephemeral—shaped by the physical capabilities of our vocal apparatus, and needing to exist, transiently, as vibrations in the air—but they have proved to be much more convenient and flexible for message transmission purposes than solid objects that must also play other roles. Talk, indeed, is cheap.

Words have also turned out to possess wonderful combinatorial properties. They can be composed in our heads to form infinitely many sentences and narratives. This enables the rapid mental formulation of ideas and plans—intellectual construction without physically doing. Thus language provides building blocks for thought, and many philosophers have argued that it also shapes or constrains thought—notably Nietzsche, who saw it as an inescapable "prisonhouse."

The residual materiality of spoken-aloud words is not entirely unimportant, though. Sometimes you have to speak up, or slow down, to get your words through to a listener. If you are sensitive to language, you will look for words that not only convey what you want to say, but also sound right. You will think of words both as carriers of information and as physical events that produce more or less pleasurable vibrations of our eardrums. If you are a lyric poet you will go even further, treating the human voice as an instrument and trying to organize words into musiclike sound structures that have internal rhymes, rhythms, and harmonies.

Written language followed the spoken version. Written words have the obvious physical advantages of persisting over time, and of being compactly storable. Written texts can therefore be lengthy, and they can easily transcend the constraints of memory—enabling the routine construction and circulation of complex narratives and arguments. Writing is not just a mechanical process of transcribing thoughts, but also serves for testing and shaping them. Similarly, reading is not simply the sequential input of text to our brains, but is often a subtle, complex process of exploring a text and considering its possible interpretations.

Written and printed words are not completely immaterial either, since they depend upon substrates, marking materials, containers—from file folders to the Library of Congress, and means of physical transportation from place to place. Graphic designers do have to take careful account of material properties, constraints, and costs when they format and produce documents. Still, a crucial benefit of written and printed messages is that they are not unnecessarily weighed down. And, as documents have evolved from inscribed tablets to parchment and eventually laser-printed pages, they have continued to shed bulk and weight.

In the particular case in numbers, it is easy to see how this process of dematerializing signifiers might have worked. According to the story usually offered by archaeologists, numbers and arithmetic began with the practice of keeping uniform physical tokens—shells, or beads, or some such—in heaps or jars to represent collections of other, bigger, heavier things, such as sacks of grain. Arithmetic was then a matter of physically adding and subtracting these tokens. (The modern abacus is a sophisticated descendent of those ancient heaps.) After a while, even lighter, more easily manipulated marks on surfaces—numerals—replaced discrete, three-dimensional tokens. From this beginning, increasingly sophisticated written notation systems evolved.

Origami and paper airplanes aside, sheets of paper exist almost entirely for the purpose of carrying information, so we tend to think of them as neutral substrates. We rarely interpret marks on paper as references to the paper itself. But when we see text, characters, and images on artifacts that serve other purposes, we generally interpret these marks as labels that *do* refer to their carriers. Natural objects do not come with labels, of course, but these days, most physical artifacts do. That is, their designers have chosen to shift part of the burden of communication from the form and materials of the artifact itself to lightweight surface symbols. So, for example, a designer of door handles might not worry about communicating their affordances through their shapes, but might simply inscribe them "push" and "pull."

In the nineteenth century, written language would have seemed to mark the end of the story. But the twentieth century unexpectedly added another chapter. It saw the emergence of electronically encoded messages—first in analog form, and then digital.

Digital information exists electromagnetically, weightlessly (unless you want to consider it at the quantum level), and invisibly. It depends for its usefulness upon devices that encode messages into that form, store them, and then decode them as required—in other words, that dematerialize and then rematerialize them. Programmable output devices such as computer displays differ dramatically from inscribed and printed artifacts since the messages that they present are not fixed, but variable.

This new surface dynamism seems unremarkable on the screens of laptop computers, which are emblematic products of the digital era and have never been any other way. But it is more startling when it destabilizes familiar things, such as the facades of buildings. As Times Square demonstrates, these can now be designed as programmable displays, so that relationships of the public faces of structures to the activities accommodated inside them can change in an instant. If you want to advertise duck on the menu, you don't even have to paint a sign, now; you can just display the message for a while.

Electronically processed bits and packets take the dematerialization of messages about as far as it can go. They cost very little to produce and process; they can be stored in immense quantities on disks and servers for practically nothing; they can be copied in an instant with no degradation; and they circulate around the world, in high-bandwidth channels, at the speed of light. They now fly through the air with the greatest of ease. The social, economic, and cultural effects of this—as became evident during the dotcom boom of the nineties—have been profound. Still, bits do not create a separate realm of cyberspace, as many argued at that time. They add a new, highly specialized, digital layer to the long-evolving, intricately interconnected system of physically functioning artifacts, spoken words, and written words.

Understandably enough, linguists, logicians, and philosophers devote most of their attention to messages in the abstract. They pay little attention to the complex interactions of these messages with the physical functionality of the artifacts that carry them. They tend to dismiss the additional functions of physically embodied messages, such as newspapers that serve for swatting flies and lighting fires, as irrelevant to their concerns. Similarly, literary theorists generally don't much care whether the texts they study appear on paper or on screen, in hardback or paperback, large type or small, as long as the messages get through.

For designers, though, it's different. They cannot ignore the specific embodiments of messages in material, potentially useful artifacts, or the potential of physically functioning artifacts also to carry messages.

From a designer's perspective, then, doing things with words is a special case of doing things with things. The limit case of language in its various lightweight and agile forms—spoken, written, and digital—has emerged from a much more solidly material, physically constraining background of artifacts and systems that must accomplish other purposes in addition to communicating.

There is insufficient evidence to support any definitive account of how this happened, but it seems likely that it occurred about 50,000 years ago, at the generally agreed dawn of human culture—perhaps, as Richard Klein has suggested, as the result of a genetic mutation. Human ancestors had made and used primitive stone tools for millions of years before that, and no doubt had communicated by means of simple sounds as well, but at this point they developed systems of artifacts of widely varied forms and functions, and they probably began to speak the sort of rapid, extensive, grammatically structured language that we would recognize as human today. In other words, they created wide ranges of different things suited to different physical and symbolic purposes, and they learned to combine these things—words to construct sentences, blades and hafts to construct axes, and eventually chunks of differently shaped materials to construct buildings.

However we may have arrived at this point, though, the communication systems that we now encounter and use in daily life clearly lie upon a pretty continuous spectrum from the densely and stubbornly material to the flexibly dematerialized, and they all work together. In any setting, there is some division of communication labor among more and less material artifacts, and among more and less physically functional compositions of them. Speaking and writing are specialized ways of making things, just as fabrication and assembly are specialized ways of saying things.

Designing is always a matter of simultaneously crafting the required functionality and the intended messages, subject to physical and economic constraints. Well-designed artifacts succeed on both levels at once. Often, today, they do so by participating in multiple systems of production, circulation, purposing and repurposing, and communication—thus forming complex hybrids, as when manufactured products carry labels and brand marks from the world of written text, and iPods serve as fashion accessories while translating downloaded digital files into audible speech and music or video displays.

Forms, themes, and conventions spawned within particular systems of artifact production, circulation, and interpretation frequently migrate to other systems and take up residence there. Architectural settings are indispensable in films and video games, for example, while film techniques and game engines now structure the presentation of architecture in computer graphics fly-throughs. These boundary crossings may seem obvious when pointed to directly, but the common critical practice of focusing exclusively upon architecture, film, product design, literature, or some other consistent category of artifacts and practices continually obscures them. Mixtures, intersections, adulterations, and contaminations of these "pure" media provide much of the density and complexity that is characteristic of today's cultural settings.

The essays in this book are snapshots, taken over several years in the middle of the first decade of the 2000s, of the now-global operation of these interwoven, inextricably dual-purpose systems of meeting practical needs and communicating by designing, producing, and circulating artifacts of diverse kinds in various combinations and hybrids. They give particular, but not exclusive emphasis to buildings and cities, and to the discourses and product ecosystems that cities support. They continue the investigation initiated in my earlier book *Placing Words*, and they have mostly appeared as regular columns in various journals.

1

KICKING THE BOTTLE

When I was a child in Australia, drinking water fell on the roof and was collected in a galvanized iron tank by the side of the house. Sometimes it had a few mosquito wrigglers, but it sufficed. Now, in Boston, my supermarket stocks bottled water from Fiji—a tinpot little military dictatorship, twelve timezones away across the Pacific Ocean. This seems unnecessary.

Our nomadic ancestors traveled to waterholes and oases, but settlement reversed the process; water began to travel to consumers. And there has always been a close connection between the water collection and distribution systems of settlements and the forms these settlements take. Since the product of water supply systems is naturally very cheap, there have also been squalid schemes to artificially inflate its price to consumers—or, in modern business school terminology, to "add value." Remember *Chinatown*?

Traditional village wells were central sources of water. Water jars served as containers for transporting it from these sources to dwellings, and donkeys and women as the vehicles. This transportation method was slow, expensive, and limited in its range, so it produced dense, focused settlement clusters. The public spaces surrounding the wells attracted people, functioned as social hubs, and provided some compelling civic imagery.

When piped water supply systems came along, this pattern fragmented and its parts recombined to generate a new kind of urban organization. Settlements were no longer so centralized, but grew out along the utility lines. Public bathing places, at the points of water availability, shattered into private bathrooms within dwellings. Wells fell into disuse, and were no longer social magnets or icons of interaction. It took a few other developments, as well, to liberate women.

Recently though, the water container has made a comeback—in updated, plastic form. Today's bottled water is really part of the late-stage hydrocarbon economy. It has a few legitimate niches—where piped water is bad or nonexistent, where buildings have insufficient plumbing, and in moving vehicles. But generally, in modern cities, you're paying a thousandfold price markup for branding, a little convenience, and maybe a very tiny, imperceptible, and unnecessary quality increment. Even worse, this distribution system adds embodied energy, transportation miles, and carbon footprint to a product that's readily available in bulk and as close to ubiquitous as anything could be.

We can recycle all those millions of bottles, of course. But the recycling process itself consumes precious space and energy, and it doesn't catch everything. The best way to take junk out of circulation is not to put it into circulation in the first place.

Whenever anyone complains that plastic-clad water is as conspicuously useless and wasteful as Paris Hilton, the beverage company flacks (sorry, reputation management professionals) swiftly do damage control. They badmouth the municipal supply, and then proudly announce that they provide a "healthy alternative" to other bottled products—neglecting to mention that the alternative has always been there for free, and that the unhealthy options are at least as vigorously pushed, with Harry Lime–like insouciance, by many of the same big, corporate, suppliers.

They're in the business of filling branded containers, and it doesn't much matter with what.

Village wells served as functional and symbolic centers for small-scale, face-to-face, local communities, but water bottles negate locality and are becoming emblems of the downsides of globalization. They fetishize distant sources that consumers never visit—essential, of course, for product differentiation and the creation of positive associations. They wouldn't exist without low-priced long-distance transportation. And they wouldn't sell without the inexpensive, ubiquitous circulation of advertising needed to create global brands.

They're perfect, in their way: useless, expensive, and bad for the planet—but marketable because they have widely recognizable labels attached to them. They are late capitalism's answer to the problem that you can't print on water itself.

2

PAPER WONDERS

The format of *Desert Island Discs* doesn't quite work for architecture. Unless you're a determinedly eccentric dotcom billionaire, it is difficult to imagine carting your eight favorite buildings off to some atoll somewhere to create your personalized Portmeirion. But the U.S. Postal Service has recently done the next best thing by issuing twelve 37-cent stamps commemorating masterworks of American modernism.

Stamps are widely circulated functional objects that also serve as miniature frames demanding pictures, so postage stamp designers are always on the lookout for discourses they can visually link to. Occasionally, architecture captures their attention.

Quick, what would *your* top twelve buildings be? There's probably some overlap with the dozen chosen by art director Derry Noyes and designer Margaret Bauer, but you will probably want to argue about a few of them. Frank Lloyd Wright is the most obvious choice. He is represented here by the Guggenheim Museum in New York, which looks considerably crisper in a postage-stamp-sized photograph than it does today in actuality—with its spalling concrete and peeling paint. The mid-century masters of steel and glass make a good showing with Mies van der Rohe's Lake Shore Apartments, Philip Johnson's Glass House in New Canaan, and the late flourish of Bruce Graham and Fazlur Khan's soaring, cross-braced Hancock Center tower in Chicago. The only other skyscraper is William Van Alen's Chrysler Building in New York—certainly iconic, but hardly modernist. Louis Kahn is there with the Exeter Academy Library, Paul Rudolph with the Yale Art and Architecture Building, and I. M. Pei with the concrete prow of the National Gallery of Art in Washington. The only really modest project in the set is Robert Venturi's Vanna Venturi house—but you can argue that it has been one of the most influential. Richard Meier's High Museum of Art in Atlanta represents classicizing late modernism. Finally, there are the free-form curves of Eero Saarinen's TWA Terminal and Frank Gehry's Disney Concert Hall.

As with the composition of haiku, space and number have traditionally imposed a rigorously minimalist discipline upon canon construction. The result, inevitably, is dispute about what's in and what's out. The Postal Service seems to relish its opportunities to engage the arguments by giving its—well, I have to say it—stamp of approval. This year, in addition to the Twelve Wonders of Modernism, it is issuing: twelve animals of the Chinese New Year; eleven Muppets; four spring flowers; twenty-seven species from North American deciduous forests; four American scientists; four distinguished Marines; ten vintage airplanes; four Disney characters; four Rio Grande blankets; ten civil rights leaders; five sporty cars; four constellations; four holiday cookies; and Henry Fonda. These stamps lead dual graphic lives as images on envelopes and as elements of carefully composed special issue sheets, with the rectangle of the printed sheet expressing the Albertian conceit that nothing could be added or taken away without screwing the whole thing up.

This sort of tastemaking is as old as history. Herodotus himself initiated the game by describing the architectural must-sees of the fifth century BC, Eastern Mediterranean world—particularly the pyramids at Giza. Later Greek authors added works constructed since the time of Herodotus, and codified the list of Seven Wonders of the World as: the

Pyramids, the Hanging Gardens of Babylon, Phidias's Statue of Zeus at Olympia, the Temple of Artemis at Ephesus, the Mausoleum of Halicarnassus, the Colossus of Rhodes, and the Pharos of Alexandria. (This was, of course, a bit like calling American ball games the World Series.) In the sixteenth century, the Dutch artist Maerten van Heemskerck solidified the idea with a series of seven marvelously fanciful engravings, and eventually, from the vantage point of baroque Vienna, Johann Fischer von Erlach published scholarly reconstructions in his history of architecture.

Latin literature has lots of references to the Seven Wonders, but Vitruvius is a conspicuous exception. He was more interested in general architectural principles than in the details of particular monuments, so he did not list his Augustan Top Ten for us. It was left to Palladio, a millennium and a half later, to travel to Rome with Vitruvius as his master and guide, to "search into the relics of all the ancient edifices, that, in spite of time and the cruelty of the Barbarians, yet remain." In his *Four Books of Architecture* he published meticulous measured drawings of some two dozen Roman temples, together with Bramante's Tempietto and his own villa and palace designs, so that his readers might learn by example to "lay aside the strange abuses, the barbarous inventions, the superfluous expense, and (what is of greater consequence) avoid the various and continual ruins that have been seen in so many fabrics." It was part *Architecture for Dummies,* part precursor to Open Source—there to be copied, and as a starting point for transformations, recombinations, corrections, and improvements.

In the education of most architects active today, the canon was represented in print by texts like Banister Fletcher's *History of Architecture*—grown fatter and fatter as its twenty editions between 1896 and 1996 struggled to cope with the increasing globalization and cross-culturalism of architectural discourse—by the classics of modernism such as Le Corbusier's *Oeuvre Complet,* and by the glossy architecture magazines. It was reinforced by the slide libraries of architecture schools, and—even more powerfully—by the slide selections of charismatic double-screen slide lecturers, like Vincent Scully at Yale. It was a far more ample canon than that conceived of by Palladio, but the restrictions of photographic and print reproduction, and the economics of publishing, kept it finite and reasonably graspable—even as a new generation of scholars was dissecting the relationship of this canon to power and ideology, and unfavorably noting its remarkable emphasis (still present in the Postal Service's top twelve) upon the more monumental works of dead, white, Western males.

Now, in our digital electronic era, everyone gets to play Desert Island iPod. With forty gigabytes in your pocket, and tens of thousands of tracks at your fingertips, this is a much less selective game than that framed by LP records and the format of a BBC radio show. The same technologies have transformed the economics of architectural images, which can now be snapped inexpensively with digital cameras, stored online or on iPods in vast quantities, and distributed through the World Wide Web by just about anyone at a tiny fraction of the cost of traditional publishing.

In this context, radical new selection mechanisms have emerged: the iPod offers random selection; items turned up by Google searches are ordered by the numbers of other sites pointing to them; and Amazon.com employs collaborative filtering to generate book recommendations. Canon construction has been taken out of the hands of scholars, critics, and publishers, and assigned to algorithms. When you next use Google Image Search to look for pictures of a building, consider this: the digital revolution has, as promised, released us from the ancient intellectual tyranny of the tastemaker and the gatekeeper—only to replace it, instantly, with the hegemony of the search engine.

3

VIVA VENTURI

Historians looking back on the era of Bush, Cheney, Rummie, and their buddies will find the cultural landscape littered with verbal coprolites—*family values, compassionate conservatism, no child left behind, healthy forests, clear skies, culture of life, people of faith,* and so on—that were readily recognizable as offensive little dollops when they were freshly dropped into public discourse, but have since hardened, through endless repetition in the media, into harmless sounding clichés. Then there are phrases like "preemptive strike," "weapons of mass destruction," "illegal combatant," and "mission accomplished" that still reek in ways that are impossible to disguise. I couldn't imagine touching these without the protection of scare quotes, the writer's equivalent of the dog-walker's plastic bag.

You're thinking what I'm thinking here, so I don't have to make direct use of the s-word in print. Like Mister Podsnap in *Our Mutual Friend,* I don't want to bring blushes to the cheeks of young architects—and I also want to avoid the attention of the ever-vigilant indecency apparatchiks. The same delicacy impels the *New York Times,* in its current bestseller list, to render the philosopher Harry Frankfurt's witty meditation on indifference to truth as *On Bull----*. This sort of typographic toilet training has its downside, though. I entered Frankfurt's title exactly as it is written in the papers, and a Google search returned the *Bulletin of the American Mathematical Society*. Then I tried it on Amazon, and got *Pit Bulls for Dummies*.

With computers, it's best simply to call a s---- a s----, but with people you can rely upon established expectations to frame your meaning. Frames, as the Berkeley linguist George Lakoff explains in *Don't Think of an Elephant*, the current cult book among America's progressive political activists, are "mental structures that shape the way we see the world." Furthermore: "All words are defined relative to conceptual frames. When you hear a word, its frame (or collection of frames) is activated in your brain." This enables you to fill in the blanks. Versions of this idea have long been current among cognitive scientists, and artificial intelligence programmers routinely employ frames as data structures for knowledge representation, but Lakoff got himself upgraded to guru class by going a step further, and suggesting: "In politics our frames shape our social policies and the institutions we form to carry out policies. To change our frames is to change all this. Reframing *is* social change." If I have made Republican policies sound like something you'd want to scrape off your shoe, I have mightily advanced the progressive cause.

Well, I'm not so sure. But Lakoff gets more interesting when he explores the relationship of frames to metaphors, and their uses in dog-whistle political rhetoric. He suggests that the master metaphor of the nation as a family frames American culture and politics. Conservatives, he says, think and act within the framework of a strict father model of the family. For them, the world is a dangerous place, stalked by evil. The role of the father (Holy, Executive Branch, or just plain Dad—but not Homer Simpson) is to protect and support the family in a difficult and threatening world, serve as a moral authority who knows right from wrong, and dish out firm punishment to wrongdoers. The role of women is to support, and the role of children is to obey. America, of course, is the father among nations, and "doesn't need a permission slip" (Bush's carefully chosen words) to act as it sees fit. Old Europe gets to be the wicked and dissolute uncle, always trying to lead the kids astray. I will leave it as an exercise for the reader to fill in the contrasting details of the kinder and gentler, gender-neutral, nurturing family model that frames things for progressives.

Reading Lakoff took me back forty years, and reminded me that one of the many merits of Robert Venturi's *Complexity and Contradiction in Architecture* was its willingness to challenge the strict father framing of architectural discourse by the leading figures of mid-century modernism. Their world, as they saw it, was full of dangerous social and aesthetic wrongs, and they were the ones to put these right. This, of course, required the rigorous discipline of the grid, structural rationality, expression of function, and less is more. These guys didn't admit women to their ranks, they didn't want to hear any backtalk from clients or users, and they didn't need any permission slips to do things their way—even when it came to lots of concrete, unloved towers, and vast urban renewal projects that obliterated old neighborhoods.

Venturi's famous book was written, he recently recalled, "as a revolutionary reaction to ideological purity and to the minimalist aesthetic and modular consistency characteristic of late Modernism." Deeply rooted in the mild, modest, and tolerant Quaker traditions of Philadelphia, attentive to the lessons of William Penn's democratic and accommodating urbanism, and published at the time of the Civil Rights and Free Speech movements, it proposed a compelling alternative to shock-and-awe modernism. It celebrated the generic vernacular loft rather than heroically original architectural expression. It stood up for pragmatic compromise and graceful accommodation of things that didn't quite fit, complex ideas rather than simplistic gestures, contradiction (which now gets disparaged as flip-flopping) and the difficult whole. Instead of making love-it-or-leave-it demands to choose between the architectural values of a high modernism imported from Europe and the vulgarities American popular culture, it voiced an ironically inflected and gently critical affection for suburbia and the commercial strip—finding them almost all right.

Now, in a timely and welcome return to print, Venturi and Denise Scott Brown have published *Architecture as Signs and Symbols*—a reflection on the practice of the firm that they have jointly headed in the decades since, and a fresh reframing of architecture for the 00s. Their starting point is the same urgent desire to shape a discourse about the future that motivated *Complexity and Contradiction*: "In the medium of architecture, if you can't do it you have to write it, and you can't do it if you are an architect ahead of your time."

Unlike the new generation of would-be strict fathers, Venturi and Scott Brown continue to see ambiguity and inconsistency as valid accommodations to the complexities and contradictions of our era. At a moment of rigidly and manipulatively framed polemical positions, they still insist on the virtues of pragmatism rather than ideology, and naughtiness rather than nuttiness. They continue, as well, to call for a generic architecture but now propose digitally controlled electronic surface as the new means to this old end.

And there's something shocking that will bring blushes to many cheeks. They insist on separating structure from symbolism. They aren't afraid to use the s-word—sign.

4

SIN NO MORE

Las Vegas was founded by gangsters, prostitutes, and real estate speculators—a good place, you'd think, to stay out of. But visitors pour through McCarran Airport in prodigious numbers; as the recent National Basketball Association All-Star Weekend in Sin City wound to a close, the check-in lines jammed every inch of the terminal and extended out the doors for blocks. The odds of making your plane were about those of hitting a slot machine jackpot, and the chances of your baggage getting on were even slimmer.

The original attraction of this hotspot in a hot desert was that there was no alternative for miles around. It began as a water stop on the trail, and then the railroad, to Los Angeles. When construction workers arrived to build nearby Hoover Dam in the thirties, and the military opened Nellis Air Force Base in the forties, it became a town to go into for a good time. Resort casinos began to pop up on what is now the older part of the Strip. By 1946, Bugsy Siegel had built the Flamingo.

Howard Hughes showed up here, by railroad car, in 1966. He moved into the Desert Inn, and a year later bought it—making the ninth floor his legendary hideaway residence. Soon, he acquired other hotels and casinos—Castaways, the New Frontier, the Landmark, the Sands, and the Silver Slipper—mostly, it seems, from the mob. To attract a new clientele, he initiated the first of the city's many image makeovers.

Shrewdly, Hughes saw that the appeal of mobster and hooker hangouts was limited, and he repackaged the Strip as a glamorous drive-to destination, with entertainment provided by the biggest names of Hollywood and national network television. Like Walt Disney with Disneyland a decade earlier, he recognized a beautiful relationship; characters and stars of the screen could market places, and in turn, suitably iconic places could market these characters.

The resulting sign-city of the late sixties—made famous among architects by the Venturi-Scott-Brown polemic *Learning from Las Vegas,* and then feared and loathed by Hunter S. Thompson—turned out to be a short-lived product of the automobile, cheap gasoline, and expansion of the highway network. It was a linear cityscape, along the ever-lengthening Strip, of vast parking lots and freestanding neon extravaganzas that were monumental enough to grab the attention of motorists speeding by.

There are still a few of these signs about, but they now seem anachronisms. They serve a diminishing purpose in an era when visitors increasingly arrive by air and are conducted immediately, by taxi or limousine, into the dark, cavernous interiors of the casino-hotels. The "Welcome to Fabulous Las Vegas" sign—improbably remaining in all its Googie glory—looks as marooned in time as a Roman city gate in a modern traffic circle. The famously erectile Dunes sign has long since succumbed to dysfunction. And, as evidenced by the Neon Museum, there is even an incipient heritage industry. Las Vegas is no longer the city of what Tom Wolfe memorably called "Boomerang Modern, Palette Curvilinear, Flash Gordon Ming-Alert Spiral, McDonald's Hamburger Parabola, Mint Casino Elliptical and Miami Beach Kidney." It has been born yet again—this time into righteousness. Hallelujah, and take up the collection!

True to its civic DNA, the repentant old show-town has made quite a spectacle of its conversion. Throughout the nineties, first-generation hotels and casinos, which were no longer putting their increasingly valuable Strip frontage to sufficiently profitable use, were theatrically blown up. It was an extended, media-friendly exorcism. First to implode was the Dunes, in 1993, to make way for today's Bellagio, followed by the unloved Landmark, the Sands of Frank, Sammy, and Dean, the Hacienda, the Aladdin, and the post-Hughes Desert Inn. It was better than fireworks, and the local television stations could put live cameras on the balconies and in the corridors. The replacements were supersized and family-friendly, with Disney-style theming out front, and a monorail around the back.

Now the Strip has become the epicenter of a traffic-choked freeway network, and relentlessly repetitive single-family housing tracts sprawl out into the desert in all directions. Lured by sunny skies, a booming local economy, and low land prices, many of each week's arrivals are planning to stay, and the metropolitan area is the fastest growing in the nation. It's generic, and it's boring. In today's marketplace, the seductions of suburbia trump sympathy for the devil.

5

LOVELIEST OF TREES

April in my garden; crocuses explode from the still snowy ground like Lilliputian antiaircraft fire aimed at the invading sun. Platoons of daffodils swiftly take over to mop up. By May Day the terrain is pacified by dazzling pear blossom; the weeping cherries and crabapples are clothed in pastels; and magnolia petals calmly litter the lawn. June sees a full-scale occupation by leafy greenery, and as the Fourth of July approaches it's all over. It's the famous Boston shock-and-awe spring.

But while the holiday flags unfurl in the early summer breeze, one tree stands tall on a nearby hill, stubbornly unchanging. It's not some sort of impassive Nordic evergreen, and it didn't die in the winter. It's a cell tower tree.

This native North American species is proliferating like prickly pear as cell-phone usage grows. It occupies its own particular ecological niche. You mostly find it where the human population is fairly dense, and where the property values are high. It prefers elevated ground with unobstructed views all round, and it typically rises well above the surrounding foliage. Just as willows cluster around water, cell tower trees go for radio frequency dead spots in the landscape—which means that they are sparsely spaced in flat country, but gather more closely among hills and valleys. Homeowners haven't yet accepted them as backyard trees, so they propagate most successfully in forests, on farms, on commercially owned land, and along highways. They are starting to sprout in graveyards, and you can see a few around Disney World in Orlando.

To the practiced eye, cell tower trees have an instantly recognizable morphology. There is an archetype, like Goethe's *Urpflanze*, underlying them all. The perfectly straight, smoothly tapered trunk is framed in metal, and it carries coaxial cables, with their sap of signals, up to the crown. There is a covering of artificial bark, formed from a polymer composite that is transparent to radio frequency radiation. The antenna elements, which are the tree's reason for being, cluster like coconuts at the very top. Branches with synthetic leaves spring from the trunk to produce well-groomed masses of green. It is all rather formal and symmetrical, more uptight Le Notre than loosey-goosey Capability Brown.

Cell-phone operators obtain their trees from suppliers such as Larson Camouflage (a division of the Larson Company, which builds faux landscapes for zoos, hotels, and theme parks), Alan Dick and Company, Preserved Treescapes International, and Stealth Concealment Solutions. They select sites and then negotiate with local zoning boards for permits. Unlike landscape designers who work with more traditional material, they face particularly pressing problems of scale and massing; heights of cell tower trees frequently extend to sixty meters or so—well into California redwood territory—but the value engineers want to limit the amount of foliage that the operators have to pay for. The result, predictably, tends to be too much trunk, with a desultory tuft of leaves at the very top. They are not so nice to sit under; no shade, and the usual base treatment is concrete footing with chain-link and razor wire enclosure and warning sign accent.

Cell tower trees come in many varieties, as appropriate to different landscape conditions. The tree degree zero is Alan Dick's lightning tree, which fits in just about anywhere. It has a few picturesquely shattered branches but no leaves, which as the catalogue notes, solves several problems: it reduces the wind load and thus the cost of the structure; it minimizes interference with antenna performance; and it means that you don't have to worry about matching the changing colors of deciduous leaves. For the desert Southwest there are some very convincing saguaro cactuses—also leafless, but with grooves and spikes. In California you see lots of palms—very efficient, since they just need a few fronds at the top, and they look great against the sunset. (Mexican fan palms are particularly popular.) In cooler climates, Scots pines and conifers seem the best bet, and their branches are particularly good at concealing a number of large-panel antennas as required for multioperator use. These efforts at verisimilitude notwithstanding, I'm pretty sure that I shall never see a cell tower lovely as a living tree.

Entirely leafless shafts, of course, give operators the most bang for their buck. They may get away with this in Nebraska, where—as the old joke has it—the state tree is a telegraph pole, but where some more determined gesture at disguise seems called for, a cell tower can pass as a flagpole. This just takes some white paint, a finial, and some fabric to flutter. It works for more urban settings, it makes NIMBY opposition seem unpatriotic, and it's cheap.

A cross can work too, provided that it is constructed from radio-frequency-friendly fiberglass. This iconographic strategy opens the way for win-win deals with churches, which tend to be centrally located in their communities, and to welcome opportunities for some additional return on their properties. I'm not too sure, though, about the metonymic coupling of Jesus with commerce, pornography, and all the generally godless stuff that flows through His Holy Emblem at 900 megahertz.

The inexorable march of the cell towers is just the latest episode in the long story that Leo Marx recounted in his classic *The Machine in the Garden*. Marx taught us to read the American landscape as the trace of repeated encounters between technology and wilderness. He recalled Henry David Thoreau, in his rural retreat at Walden Pond, hearkening to the whistle of the "devilish Iron Horse" echoing through the springtime woods, and he observed that many subsequent writers had constructed similar scenes to suggest simultaneously the unstoppable progress of the industrial revolution and the loss of pastoral innocence. What is striking, when you read them today, is their frequent use of comically sexualized language that seems to anticipate Philip Roth. The powerful locomotive pants and shrieks and thrusts. Nature submits.

Now that the age of steam has long gone, and telecommunication towers have become the latest avatars of technological progress, the uneasy couplings of machine and garden continue. But the machine has come out as a cross-dresser, and the garden isn't quite what it seems.

6

ALBERTI'S ANNIVERSARY

The year 2005 saw Alberti's 600th birthday. To celebrate, there was a splendid exhibition entitled "Rome of Leon Battista Alberti" at the Palazzo Caffarelli on the Capitoline Hill. It began at a breezy window providing a wide view of the city itself. On the floor below there was a carefully aligned map, and on the adjacent wall some text from Alberti's short Latin work *Panorama of the City of Rome.*

This mise-en-scène recalled the famous moment in the 1440s when the ambitious young humanist and antiquarian surveyed the city from a nearby tower. Not for him the subjective sketch; his method was resolutely scientific. Employing an instrument of his own devising—essentially a disk divided around the rim into 48 degrees, with a graduated ruler pivoting at the center—he plotted the precise polar coordinates of walls, gates, churches, and other prominent landmarks. He did not go on to draft and publish a map, as one might expect, but instead provided his readers with the resulting tables of numbers. In other words, he gave them a cartographic database. Just by reading the *Panorama,* he boasted, "anyone, even if of only modest intelligence" could construct his own, accurate picture of the city "on whatever surface he wishes." Alberti was doing computer graphics before the computer.

The year 2005 also saw the emergence of online, global cartographic databases. These digital counterparts of Alberti's tables contain orders of magnitude more numbers, and their coding schemes are a bit trickier, but their essential logic is pretty much the same. With the aid of the associated software, anyone, even if of only modest computer skills, can use them to map any city on whatever screen he wishes. It's *Panorama* for dummies.

Google Maps, for example, now allows users to range over the entire surface of the Earth. You can view either constructed street maps or detailed satellite images of the areas you alight upon. In seconds, if you wish, you can open a virtual window over the Capitoline Hill and plot the same ancient landmarks that presented themselves to Alberti. With Google Earth, you can perform even more impressive maneuvers.

There are also many competing systems. All the usual suspects are in the game. Microsoft is touting MSN Virtual Earth, and Yahoo has Yahoo Maps. NASA's World Wind is an open source, downloadable virtual Earth with associated software tools. Amazon's A9 provides access not only to maps but also to tens of millions of geographically indexed street-level photographs of businesses—the distant, digital descendents of the street-level perspectives comprising Piranesi's *Views of Rome.*

Unlike printed maps, online mapping systems don't require you to view a city at a particular, fixed scale and level of detail. Giambattista Nolli, for example, chose a generous scale that enabled him to show a great deal of fascinating architectural detail on his great eighteenth-century map of Rome, but this made the whole thing unwieldy; he had to divide it into twelve large sheets. Digitally displayed maps escape the limitations of fixed scale by providing software for panning and zooming over virtual surfaces of vast extent. As long as you have a sufficiently fast link to the database and a sufficiently powerful processor, this technique allows you instant access to maps of all the places in all the world, in all the detail you might want, on even the tiny, mobile screens of cell phones and PDAs.

Furthermore, digital maps can be programmed to show their own locations. This sort of self-reference was first provided in the GPS navigation systems of ships and aircraft, soon spread to automobile navigation systems, and is now ready to jump into your pocket. If your cell phone cannot already tell you exactly where you are, it soon will. Its screen will display maps that automatically register your current coordinates on them, and it will become your indispensable urban guide. Furthermore, it will automatically attach spatial coordinates as well as time stamps to the digital photos you snap with it—constructing an ongoing record of the places you inhabit and the people you encounter, and allowing you virtual revisits simply by specifying the places and dates you want.

Google Maps and the like would be useful, but of limited cultural interest, if they merely offered passive viewing. But they come with APIs (application program interfaces) that allow programmers to create overlays of data drawn from other sources—particularly other web sites—and this has spawned the popular new practice of making map mash-ups. These are the cartographic equivalents of mid-00s mash-up music such as DJ Danger Mouse's *Gray Album*, which digitally melds tracks from the Beatles' *White Album* with hip-hop artist Jay-Z's *Black Album* to amazing effect and the fury of the Beatles' label's lawyers.

One of the first map mash-ups to attract attention was housingmaps.com, which pulls data from Craig's List and on Google Maps shows locations of apartments for sale and rent. Another early hit was chicagocrime.org, which gets its data from the Chicago police web site and plots crime locations—filtered by date and category of offense—in the Windy City. One of my personal favorites is fundrace.org, which trawls through campaign contribution records to map where political money comes from. The last time I looked, I found map mash-ups showing the locations of live webcams in various cities, current residences of convicted sex offenders in Georgia, recent earthquakes, recent UFO sighting reports, World Heritage sites (with photographs that pop up when you click the corresponding locations), and the homes of America's Iraq War casualties.

The Rome that Alberti surveyed from his tower, and so avidly sought to learn from, was an urban *Gray Album*—a complex layering onto the seven hills of ancient monuments, medieval churches, and an emerging renaissance city. Recent buildings had been mashed onto the foundations of older ones, churches had been built inside the shells of temples, and ancient stones had been recombined to produce new structures. The Global Village that we can now survey from our virtual vantage points is an equally complex and impure cyberspace mash-up, constructed by layering an astonishing diversity of data onto a virtual Earth.

These layers form an accumulating digital sediment. As newer layers supplant them, they will fall into disuse and ruin. Eventually, perhaps, the Albertis of the future will devise instruments of cyberspace archaeology and excavate them to recover and interpret the world as it was at the dawn of 2006.

7

THE NET HAS A THOUSAND EYES

Remember those desktop videophones that the telephone companies promoted for decades? They were an unsuccessful product mutation, a dead-end branch in the evolutionary tree of electronic devices—and the reason is obvious; they put the eyes of the network in the wrong places. A representation of the visible world constructed from the viewpoints of desk accessories just wasn't that interesting.

The Webcams that emerged during the Internet boom of the 1990s were a little more engaging. You could point them out the window, and so make your contribution to an online collection of low-resolution panoramic views that changed with the sun, the weather, and urban activity patterns—an increasingly dense, ongoing global portrait available at any networked computer. Or you could deploy them in otherwise private space to engage in some novel forms of electronically mediated exhibitionism, peeping-Tommery, and pornography. These days, if you do a Google search on Webcam, you get tens of thousands of hits, with Webcam index sites heading the list. For all that, Webcam surfing has remained a fairly marginal subcultural practice, like ham radio operation.

By contrast, tiny digital cameras in cell phones were an instant success. Their proliferation attached millions of mobile observation points to the Internet, and this immediately initiated a popular new form of visual discourse. In the process of evolving a global digital sensorium, the camera-phone mutation has turned out to be a winner.

The camera-phone continues by other means a trend toward image mobilization that began, long ago, with the shift from painting on walls to making pictures on small pieces of wood, canvas, or paper. Disengaged images were transportable, so practices of distribution and trade, accumulation in collections and books, and display in galleries and other specialized locations, were able to emerge. In the great age of exploration, the topographic draftsmen who accompanied expeditions recorded images of distant places and carried them back to the imperial capitals to construct an increasingly comprehensive representation of a wide world out there awaiting colonization, scientific investigation, and the word of God.

With the industrial technologies of photography, high-speed printing, and rapid transportation, the global system of image production, accumulation, and distribution increased its speed and scale by orders of magnitude. Over the century and a half during which silver halide held sway, associated image systems evolved into a variety of specialized variants. Inexpensive consumer cameras combined with photofinishing services and family albums to establish a domestic image cycle. Topographic photography, printing, and mail services yielded the picture postcard. Photojournalism, wire services, and newspaper and magazine publishing jointly produced the mass-circulation illustrated news story. The circulation of mug shots and crime-scene photographs, and the accumulation of image archives transformed police work. Photographic emulsion and the practices of the eyewitness formed a powerful alliance, based on the doubtful but widely accepted proposition that the camera didn't lie.

With the introduction of the camera-phone, the image production, accumulation, and distribution system began to operate entirely digitally, and with unprecedented efficiency. Images could now be captured by ubiquitous mobile devices, wirelessly transmitted to servers that accumulated image databases, redistributed through global networks, and almost immediately displayed on cell phone, PDA, and computer screens throughout the world. Furthermore, they often came with metadata that enabled instant sorting and searching of large collections—time and date of creation for a start, geographic coordinates as cell phones became location-sensitive, and even more as additional forms of context-sensitivity were added. By dematerializing images, eliminating mechanical and chemical processes from their life cycles, and forming tight electronic linkages between production and distribution stages, the camera-phone has fully disengaged visual information from its material substrates, and speeded its flow as never before.

The result is a new Panopticon—not the architectural sort as proposed by Bentham, nor even the more subtle and insidious kind that we were confronted with by Foucault, but a consumer-electronics version. Anywhere you happen to be, at any time, there's probably someone around with a camera-phone, and a record of your activities might instantly end up on the Web. It is not the thought of a central, invisible observer that increasingly disciplines us under this condition, but the realization that anyone with a personal computer and a search engine can stealthily make us objects of surveillance. Maybe it's fine when awareness of the tireless electronic gaze restrains the behavior of police at street demonstrations, but it's less comforting to know that terrorists, spooks, and stalkers can surf the Web like all the rest of us.

This reconfigured, accelerated system of visual recording and presentation also redistributes power to control the flow of images. The printing press, in particular, has traditionally been a point of centralized control; a few photo-editors have determined what we see in the papers, and the censor's job has been all too easy. But every camera-phone now has instant access to the global digital network, anonymous remailers can conceal the origins of images, mailing lists and email forwarding can provide vast distribution for practically nothing. And, as with music, peer-to-peer exchange of image files provides an increasingly robust alternative to more familiar, centrally controlled distribution strategies. Once you have introduced a digital image into the global network it can multiply and spread like a virus, and effective suppression is very difficult. Once the notorious Abu Ghraib torture pictures were out on the Internet, there was no way to reel them back in. Bloggers, pornographers, spammers, pranksters, blackmailers, whistle-blowers, and political protestors have quickly learned this lesson.

At the point of capture, camera-phones induce some particularly subtle and ambiguous body language. A traditional camera is a highly recognizable item that signals your intention to take pictures. It is emblematic; when you choose to carry one it clearly casts you in the role of photographer. The gesture of raising it to your eye indicates that an exposure is imminent, and the sound of the shutter confirms that the job is done. But a camera-phone is always there in your pocket or handbag, and its ostensible purpose is something different. Even to a close observer, snapping a picture is generally indistinguishable from dialing a number, sending a text message, or surfing the Web, and unless an electronic click has been specially added, there is no telltale shutter sound. Picture taking has become almost undetectable. So, increasingly, you are required to turn off, pocket, or even hand over phones in locker rooms, at confidential briefings, and where there are security sensitivities.

It is tempting to think of the miniaturized digital camera and the camera-phone as descendents of Cartier-Bresson's Leica, always at the ready to frame, snap, and capture a decisive moment. To some extent this is true. When photographers substitute digital single-lens reflex cameras for their 35 mm film predecessors, the resulting images are often visually indistinguishable from those shot on film; they are high-resolution, and framed and exposed in much the same way. But the camera-phone has no conventional viewfinder, it is typically held at arms-length to snap an image, and it produces images fitted to the capabilities of its tiny, low-resolution screen. (It is as if your eye were shifted to the palm of your hand, and provided a much narrower view angle.) These technical differences are altering conventions of framing—privileging the tight, radically cropped close-up over more classical and expansive compositional modes—much as television's smaller, fuzzier screen induced tighter framing and faster editing from that of the cinema.

Since exposures are very cheap, and made at points displaced from the photographer's eye, compositions are often quite casual, and embedded in sequences rather than existing in isolation. There are some precedents for this in photographic practice. One thinks, for example, of Gary Winogrand's obsessive snapping in the street, of the New York subway pictures that Walker Evans made between 1938 and 1941—clandestinely, from beneath his winter coat, in violation of a ban on subway photography—and those made by Helen Levitt, who used a right-angle viewfinder to conceal what she was up to. But the camera-phone has pumped up what was, with earlier technologies, mostly a suppressed potential. Often, the images produced by camera-phones seem less like products of the photographer's authorial intentions and explicit artistic choices than traditional photographs, and more like random samples extracted from the continuous flow of visual experience.

In fact, the natural mode of the camera-phone is not the single frame but the sequence of frames—the short digital video clip. Such clips can be played as the motion equivalents of snapshots—slices of life a few seconds long, they can be mined for telling still images, and they can function as mobile, inexpensive, readily recombinant audiovisual fragments. The sequences of frames produced by surveillance cameras and Webcams are even further displaced from the photographic tradition of framing and snapping at decisive moments—producing compositions that, at least for purists, were not to be subsequently cropped or otherwise manipulated. When still images or short motion sequences are extracted from Webcam data streams, the context of artistic or journalistic choice shifts from the time and place of the action, with the photographer in the role of eyewitness on the spot, to spatially and temporally shifted computational settings in which editors sort, search, select from, and perhaps transform and recombine visual data.

Since the development of fast film emulsions and camera shutters, we have tended to think of photographs as instantaneous; effects such as motion blur, double exposures, and the frozen look of old photographic portraits made with long exposures were deviations from the norm. But a digital camera may make several exposures in very quick succession, then automatically combine the resulting frames to achieve better tonal rendition. Frames taken at longer intervals may be processed, in a different way, to remove moving foreground objects. Frames taken from a moving viewpoint may be combined, through a process of matching common but displaced features in successive exposures, to produce three-dimensional digital models that can then be renavigated, in real time, in arbitrary ways. Frames showing faces may be averaged to produce statistical reference faces for use by face recognition systems—which look for telling deviations from the reference face. In all of these cases, images are constructed algorithmically from the raw digital data.

The digital images that are produced and distributed in these ways are not closed and finalized within their frames. They do not present themselves to us as untouchable works of art, like Renaissance paintings or Edward Weston prints, but as incomplete data fragments, like DNA sequences, inviting endless mutation and recombination into larger information structures. And new digital tools and practices have emerged to support this. To Photoshop has become a transitive verb. The PowerPoint file has become the unit of discourse in the classroom and conference room, driving to extinction the 35 mm slide carousel. Bloggers and photologgers combine images and text online, and have reinvented the diary and the sketchbook. During the 2004 U.S. Presidential Election season, the JibJab motion collages "This Land," and "Good to Be in DC," were huge, server-crashing hits of the constructed digital graphics genre. But all this has come at a price; as practices of image manipulation have proliferated, the photograph's claim to unquestionable veracity has correspondingly faded.

The Internet, with ever-multiplying digital cameras, Webcams, and camera-phones serving as its eyes, has now evolved into an almost incomprehensively vast, pervasive system for extracting visual information from the world and efficiently preserving it. The resulting, explosively expanding, online image collection has succeeded the picture gallery, the illustrated book, and the photographic and print "museum without walls" as our era's characteristic form of image accumulation, organization, and presentation. Personal computers and search engines provide access to just about anything that it contains, anywhere, anytime, for anyone. The viewer's role is not confined to the hands-off gaze, but often involves active appropriation, transformation, and recombination of image content, then redistribution of the results through the same digital channels, so that the distinction between producers and consumers becomes hopelessly blurred. A continuously operating, geographically distributed, multiway observation and memory machine has supplanted the singular artist's viewpoint of Renaissance perspective, and the frozen moment of the photographic exposure.

8

SURVEILLANCE COOKBOOK

Imagine being one of Big Brother's Thought Police—the 1984 kind, not the sort that reality television cunningly casts couch potatoes as. In between the juicy thought crimes you were supposed to be snooping for, you'd have to gaze endlessly upon the tediously quotidian. It would be like sitting through an Andy Warhol movie without the drugs.

Of course, according to the celebrated argument advanced by Michel Foucault, you wouldn't have to keep your eyes glued to the screen *all* the time. The mere presence of the surveillance apparatus, and the realization that the Thought Police *might* be watching, would be enough to keep everyone intimidated. Still, as a communications engineer might say, Big Brother would run into a serious signal-to-noise ratio problem if he were actually trying to gather actionable intelligence. And, after a while, his spooks would start going postal. I guess Orwell didn't think about scalability.

Here, then, are my tips on how to overcome the difficulty and set up a cutting-edge, cost-effective surveillance state. For ambitious political leaders who haven't yet figured it out, the following step-by-step instructions can serve as a sort of *Anarchist's Cookbook*. (Don't look that up online, though; the National Security Agency may be monitoring downloads.) Each of these moves will seem reasonable and innocuous, and with luck, nobody will connect the dots.

First of all, don't go to the trouble of creating and deploying your own surveillance devices. This is an expensive strategy, and it only arouses suspicion and resistance. Outsource instead. Let existing businesses and institutions—which generally have the motivations and the means to compile databases for their internal purposes—do it for you.

You should, for instance, take full advantage of electronic access control technology. I'm not paranoid, really I'm not, but I know that the building containing my office is already tracking me. It has a card-key system that logs everyone entering the front door, everyone going to each floor, and exact entry times. This is convenient, and right now it doesn't seem intrusive; the logs are kept for just two weeks, and there are very strict controls on who gets access to them. But the electronic surveillance infrastructure is there, at no cost to the government, and policies can always be changed. And future upgrades for RFID bracelets and implanted identification chips will be easy.

Out in the street, I'm invisibly followed. Whenever I use Oyster Card payment on London public transport, for example, it traces my movements through the system. Whenever I drive on toll roads or enter parking structures, transponders in my car communicate with wireless readers to register my presence in order to charge me for it. In some locations, license plate recognition cameras record every vehicle that goes by for purposes of extracting tolls, applying the London Congestion Charge, or automatically generating speeding tickets. Increasingly, as the technology improves, CCTV cameras in the streets will automatically check my face against their watch lists.

The logs of cellular telephone providers have long recorded every move I make. They track not only times of calls and numbers dialed, but also the locations of my phone whenever it is switched on. In the European Union, the Data Retention Directive of 2005 requires telecommunications providers to retain their records for extended periods, and to place them at the disposal of governmental bodies. In the United States, as *USA Today* recently revealed, the NSA has enlisted the cooperation of the big phone companies, without warrants, to compile a massive database of calling records. And, in any case, there are Web sites that will sell you anyone's phone records.

These days, in fact, just about all human activities leave potentially telling traces in databases somewhere. The information you need for total surveillance is all there; you just have to get access to it. Admittedly, this can present some challenges. The owners of data may be reluctant to provide it to you—generally not for ethical reasons, but because they don't want to get sued by their customers. And civil libertarians will certainly resist. But you can always respond indignantly that 9/11 and the London bombings changed everything; in a world infested with terrorists, you are just taking necessary steps to protect your citizens from foreigners who want to kill them. Furthermore, busybody scrutiny of your activities just aids the enemy. If that doesn't suffice, you can play the child protection card; just claim that you're in relentless pursuit of pornographers.

Your systems programmers will then need to match individuals across different databases. They will have to be able to establish, for example, that the Bill Mitchell who bought a subversive sounding book on Amazon, the William Mitchell who made a call to Pakistan on his T-Mobile phone, and the fellow caught by a surveillance camera closely eying the new Foster skyscraper in Manhattan were one and the same. If you think you can get away with it, you can try to push through the creation of a national ID card system, and then insist on the universal use of unique identification numbers in computer records. That's a nice, clean technical solution to the data collation problem, but it forces you to show your hand. With less public fuss, you can simply get your programmers to construct tables that quietly do the necessary matching.

You will now have a mountain of data to sift through, but that's no problem for advanced search technology. As Google has demonstrated, you need software that continually crawls through the data to index it.

This sort of software is increasingly capable of handling not only online text, but also email, recorded telephone conversations (in which keywords are automatically recognized), images, and motion events in surveillance videos. As soon as you have constructed a good index, you can get instant answers to your queries. Better yet, you can go data mining, electronically pursue leads, and program your system to look for suspicious coincidences, sequences, clusters, and patterns—*Minority Report*'s precrime without those creepy mutants in vats.

If you get complaints about illegal spying on innocent citizens, you should respond that you're simply tracing links with known bad guys—and what could be wrong with that? Technically, you will be correct. In the vast, dense web of linkages that your database establishes, everyone will be connected to just about everyone else—including real criminals—with surprisingly few degrees of separation. If I happen to order takeout from the same restaurant as a terrorist mastermind, then network analysis of the phone records will show that I'm just two links away from him.

Follow these tips and, like today's most innovative businesses—Dell and Qualcomm, for example—you will have organized a modern, nimble system of independent suppliers. You will be able to focus your own efforts upon coordination, supply-chain management, and harvesting value by means of state-of-the-art software. That's way ahead of Big Brother's cumbersome, old-fashioned state bureaucracy. You could get written up in the *Economist*—maybe even become a Harvard Business School case.

9

FORGET FOREIGN WARS

For a networked, global city there is no such thing as a foreign war.

The walled cities of earlier times certainly seemed to clarify things, especially when they were run by despots. You could reasonably assume that the good guys were inside, the bad guys were outside, and you mounted your defenses at the unambiguous dividing line. If you weren't with us, you were against us. But open, cosmopolitan, tolerant cities like London, New York, and Paris are the greatest achievements of our globalizing era, and we now urgently confront the question of how to defend them effectively without destroying the very qualities that make them so valuable and wonderful.

It is a commonplace of urban history that the development of explosives rendered city walls obsolete. This is, indeed, part of the story. When artillery can lob destruction through the air, and bombers can fly overhead, walls are ineffective defenses. They would not have helped London during the Blitz, Hiroshima, Dresden, or the victims of shock-and-awe in Baghdad. But, as economies became more sophisticated and cities grew more interdependent, the walls also *needed* to come down to facilitate interchange and trade. In an increasingly networked world, closed cities simply don't thrive. Look at Pyongyang.

The most actively interconnected nodes within global transportation and telecommunication networks have clearly become the economic, intellectual, and cultural hotspots of today's world. The connections of these centers to one another are at least as important as the connections to their traditional, often much more conservative hinterlands. They are the sites of crucial business transactions, magnets for talent, hothouses of innovation and creativity, and loci of influence and power. They are the great global cities—maybe thirty or forty of them.

It depends a bit on how you measure, but a recent study by Loughborough University's Globalization and World Cities group plausibly has the top twenty global cities—measured by their levels of global network connectivity—as London, New York, Hong Kong, Paris, Tokyo, Singapore, Chicago, Milan, Los Angeles, Toronto, Madrid, Amsterdam, Sydney, Frankfurt, Brussels, Sao Paulo, San Francisco, Mexico City, Zurich, and Taipei. It comes as no surprise that there are no representatives from the former Soviets, the tyrant-ridden zones of the Middle East, or the red states of the United States. The list includes many of the places most reviled by backwoods demagogues of all stripes—from Osama in his cave to Pennsylvania's unspeakable Senator Santorum—as hotbeds of permissiveness, refusal of censorship, indifference to traditional family values, and skepticism about the strictures of old-time religion. And they are all crawling with damned foreigners.

The global cities have a lot in common. Generally they are centers of populous, economically vibrant metropolitan areas that include diverse cultures and communities. They attract worldwide attention, are much visited, and participate actively in international affairs. They have major international airports, advanced transportation and telecommunications infrastructures, financial institutions, courts and law firms, corporate headquarters, leading medical facilities, serious universities and research centers, and renowned cultural institutions. Their cultural, entertainment, and sporting scenes are lively, and their media outlets are influential. They are fascinating and seductive, they are much envied, and they turn out to be very vulnerable to violent attack by those who hate the liberal-minded, outward-looking, secular modernity that they so vividly and successfully represent.

This inherent vulnerability results from their necessary permeability to global flows of people, materials, and information, from their embedding in far-flung transportation, water and energy supply, and information networks that can be shut down or hijacked with disconcerting ease, and from their dependence upon high levels of trust among their inhabitants. There is no one line of defense. As we have so sadly seen, each of the global cities becomes a scattered collection of thousands of potential targets when viewed through resourcefully hostile eyes. Even worse, the effects of attacks on these targets are not just local but can propagate widely throughout urban networks and the social and economic systems that depend upon them.

Under these conditions, macho blather about axes of evil, wars on terrorism, and rooting out villains obviously doesn't help. Furthermore, it is foolish to allocate precious resources to attacking conveniently distant and nasty nations. Some judicious tightening of borders is probably sensible, but terrorists aren't necessarily foreigners and foreigners certainly aren't necessarily terrorists, and it quickly becomes self-defeating for globally connected communities to inhibit the free flow of talent and ideas and to reinforce patterns of mistrust and hostility among racial and religious groups. Too narrow a focus on defending major centers merely displaces hostile attention to more convenient surrogates like Sharm el-Sheikh, Kusadasi, Bali, and Oklahoma City. The problem is too pervasive, diffuse, and deeply rooted for any of this.

We should face up to the hard truth that global cities, by their very nature, will *always* face some irreducible risk of attack from unexpected corners of the networked world—including from within themselves. We can and must work to eliminate the causes of murderous urban attacks and move decisively against the perpetrators, but, in an interconnected world replete with motives, means, and opportunities, we will no more eliminate the ongoing possibility than we will eliminate natural hazards like fires and earthquakes.

One part of the necessary response, then, is to avoid the futilities of panic, xenophobia, and demagoguery, and dispassionately to play the probabilities instead. Defenders of cities (including designers of buildings and public spaces) can estimate the likelihoods of attack on potential targets, factor in the magnitudes of the likely outcomes, and use the results to guide the allocation of available defensive resources. It sounds coldly calculating, and it is. But this will generate a statistically distributed bulwark, with a strength that can vary according to the state of the world, the resources available, and the levels of risk that citizens are willing to bear. In our ambiguous, uncertain, inextricably interconnected world, it is the imperfect best that they can do.

The other part—now more than ever—is a fierce commitment, by their citizens, to the ideals and freedoms that have made the global cities what they are. If these cities can be intimidated—either by those who attack them or more insidiously by those who claim to be taking measures that are necessary for their defense—into retreating from their characteristic openness, tolerance, diversity, and intellectual and cultural adventurousness, then the ignorant thugs who have the effrontery to pass off their bigotry as morality will have won the day.

10

EVERYDAY LOW

The only thing that kept me in the theater through Steven Spielberg's numbingly boring *War of the Worlds* was the vain hope of seeing Tom Cruise get stomped by one of those spindly-legged tripod things. But the images of cratered-out communities did hammer home the point that ruthless, alien invaders can be an awfully bad thing for a town.

They made me think wistfully of a more innocent time, long ago, before the arrival of the big boxes. No one would have believed in the last decades of the twentieth century that Small Town America was being watched keenly and closely by creatures with retail expansion in mind. Yet across the gulf of cornfields and cow country, minds that were to the minds of the locals as theirs were to those of the beasts that perish, intellects vast and cool and unsympathetic, regarded Main Streets with envious eyes, and slowly and surely drew their plans against them. (Well, that's the spin that the *Economist* and *Fast Company* put on it.) They came from Bentonville, Arkansas. They were the Wal-Martians.

The giant Wal-Mart Corporation was neither the first nor is it the only box-in-a-parking-lot retailer in the United States—Kmart, Target, Home Depot, and Costco are among its competitors—but it is the biggest, baddest, and currently the most embattled. Like the tripods from the Red Planet, Wal-Mart seemed invincible at first. It expanded inexorably across the country by targeting vulnerable small towns, and then picking them off one by one. The lack of strong, nation-wide planning codes made this easy. The Bentonville advance guard went in with a three-part siren song of "everyday low prices" for the cash-strapped customer, entry-level jobs for the unemployed, and property taxes for local government. If local planners or citizen activists resisted, then Wal-Mart simply squished them with well-financed campaigns run by their PR flacks (sorry, reputation managers), together with the suggestion that standing in the way was un-American, an affront to the spirit of cornpone capitalism, and downright communistic.

Pretty soon a big box had landed like a spaceship on the edge of town. The unions were seen off, the local merchants were out of business, and Main Street was shuttered and deserted. The jobs turned out to pay poorly, and net employment in the area generally went down once the local businesses were gone, but by the time anyone figured that out it was too late. It was a zero-sum game. The big box did nothing to expand the local economy (as, say, a new manufacturing facility might), but simply took control and the profits out of town. Meanwhile, Wall Street rejoiced, and the folksy founder Sam Walton became the subject of inspirational volumes in the business sections of airport bookstores.

Wal-Mart has a well-deserved reputation for shrewd management, innovative use of information technology, and brilliant organization of its global supply network. Where it brings discount retailing to low-income areas that had previously been poorly served, as it did recently in South Central Los Angeles, it performs a genuine service. But the Wal-Martians in charge refuse to be held back by scruples—the unaffordable, sentimental baggage of losers. So containing payroll costs becomes holding wages down to poverty levels, skimping on employee health benefits (shifting the burden to the public sector), understaffing stores, routinely violating immigration and labor laws, discriminating against women, and viciously fighting unions. Global sourcing becomes connection of the world's worst sweatshops and child labor exploiters—under cover of innocuous-looking logos and labels—to the huge American market. And the search for expansion opportunities becomes an endless sequence of site fights—all-out battles to overcome community opposition, break local planning controls, and force big boxes into communities that don't need or want them.

The Bentonville behemoth depends upon its scale advantage to maintain an edge over its competitors, and it is driven by the inflated expectations of cheerleading Wall Street analysts, so it must either continue to grow or die. It cannot stop looking for new worlds to wage war on. Just as Spielberg's metal-clad monsters set their sights on our green and pleasant planet, then, the predatory box-builders have now moved on to picking site fights in urban America, Europe, and Asia. Here, the opposition turns out to be more sophisticated and effective. Wal-Mart has recently lost a bitter battle to build a store on Queens Boulevard in New York, for example, and the coalition of unions, local retailers, and civil activists that stopped it has gone on to campaign for city council action that would effectively bar the retailer from the five boroughs for good. Where Spielberg showed his invaders landing amid thunderbolts on a suburban shopping street in New Jersey, *New York* magazine—never to be outdone in the sensational image department—illustrated its report with a special effects photomontage of a Wal-Mart landing among the elegant storefronts on Fifth Avenue. Run, Tom Cruise, run!

In addition to this now-famous Battle of Rego Park, there have been brutal and expensive site fights in Chicago and Los Angeles. When Wal-Mart could not get planning permission to build a store in Inglewood, California—a gritty, mostly minority suburban city near Los Angeles International Airport—it sponsored a ballot initiative that would have exempted it from all planning controls. Its forces spent a lot of money and campaigned hard, but eventually lost by a wide margin. This working-class community was unimpressed by the slick corporate salesmen, and it ran them out of town.

10

From the particular professional perspective of the architects and urban designers who have joined these fights, the trouble with big boxes is not so much that they are crudely conceived and shoddily constructed—usually nothing more than standardized, system-built, fluorescently lit enclosures that have been value-engineered down to the bare minimum—but that they trash the ancient and mutually beneficial alliance between commerce and public space. Market squares served simultaneously as spaces for merchants and meeting places for the citizens who were attracted by them. So did commercial Main Streets and High Streets, both at the village scale and in their industrial-era extensions along public transportation routes. The great urban department stores added to the vitality of downtowns. Even suburban shopping malls (particularly as pioneered by Victor Gruen) have typically been built around the best facsimiles of real public space that their designers can manage. But big boxes in oceans of asphalt on the edges of towns are not even bothering to try—and furthermore, they displace the alternatives. They are machines for reducing citizens to consumers.

In Spielberg's movie, the invaders come to a sticky end. For all their vast intelligence, these imagined Martians didn't count on Earthly microbes. Maybe the Wal-Martians, for all their Southern-fried Schumpeterian triumphalism, haven't really understood price. Perhaps they haven't counted on the deadly effects of rising gasoline prices on cars in parking lots. You never know.

11

TEXAS CHAIN STORE

Places for selling food have always been shaped both by the rituals of daily urban life and by the increasingly extended networks connecting towns and cities to agricultural sites in the countryside. With the opening of a vast new Whole Foods supermarket on London's Kensington High Street—an exclusive Foodistan proclaiming its observance of strict organic law—a new species of urban space is emerging.

Things have changed fast. I grew up, not so very long ago, in a small country town with old-fashioned food stores lining the Main Street: the butcher, the baker, the grocer, and the greengrocer. (We were on the electrical grid, so the candlestick maker was gone—to return, decades later, as a high-priced boutique with scented products for tourists.) In the absence of an extensive, refrigerated transportation network, these small, independent businesses mostly found their supplies in the surrounding region; food with a lot of miles on it wasn't an option. The exception was the grocer, who carried a few exotic, nonperishable packaged items like Vencatachellum's Mild Madras Curry Powder.

Food shopping, under this arrangement, was a daily pedestrian activity—mostly conducted by housewives, who were presumed to have the time for it during daylight hours. The display windows of the stores formed a continuous street facade, and they presented what was in season and available at that moment. You knew when the local strawberries had ripened, and when the butcher had just slaughtered a beast. It was a primitive system by today's standards, and I wouldn't want to defend the social assumptions that supported it, but it represented the traditional relationship between town and countryside with vivid and beautiful clarity.

Today's big-box supermarkets, by contrast, represent a globalized world. Their supply chains extend to the ends of the earth. Since just about anything, at any moment, is available somewhere within reach of them, seasonality is mostly indicated by price; I can get strawberries almost anytime at my local supermarket, but the cost drops, with the approach of summer, as the fields where they ripen become closer. Other offerings are complex manufactured food products created, in stages, by networks of production facilities—much like automobiles or laptop computers. These have indefinite origins in space and time; the mightily defended French concept of *terroir* certainly doesn't apply to them, and you have to worry whether a can of dog food contains, as one of its many constituents, gluten that was adulterated in some Chinese city you never heard of.

The supermarket's style of representation originated in earlier ages of discovery and colonization. It derives from cabinets of curiosities, museums, botanical gardens, zoos, and the great world expositions, in which each collected and displayed item served as a synecdoche for its place of origin. By collecting from everywhere, the citizens of colonial capitals could encapsulate the whole wide world in bounded spaces, and so express their mastery over it. Similarly, the shelves of well-stocked, high-end supermarkets don't just provide a lot of consumer choice; they also meet a psychic need—comfortably reassuring customers that they are on top of the globally networked heap.

With its carefully staged displays, performances, and themed eateries, London's new Whole Foods—like the stores the Texas-based chain has recently opened in New York—is in the psychic need business in a bigger way than ever before. The food is pretty good, but it's hardly unique, and the prices are high. You're paying for self-referential theater—for a well-produced show in which *you* star as sophisticated citizen of a great, powerful, global city.

12

RIGHT PLACE AT THE WRONG TIME

"I been in the right place, but it must have been the wrong time." I couldn't get it out of my head. The cheerful rhythm of Dr. John's funky old song recalled the good-time town that everyone loved, but the words seemed sickeningly ominous as hurricane refugees fled to the Superdome.

Before Katrina, New Orleans was the right place for many things. It was the right place for African, Caribbean, and Creole cultures to take hold and flourish. It was the right place for musicians like Louis Armstrong, Jelly Roll Morton, Fats Domino, Professor Longhair, Dr. John, Wynton Marsalis, and countless others to develop their distinctive sounds. It was the right place for William Faulkner and Tennessee Williams to come to write, and for Williams to set the drama of Stanley and Blanche. It was the right place for the elegant, airy simplicity of shotgun and dogtrot houses, and for the over-the-top exuberance of Charles Moore's Piazza d'Italia. It was as good a place as any, for a while, for William Burroughs (who hung out across the river in Algiers), Jack Kerouac, and Neal Cassady.

It was the one Southern place—as Howell Raines observed in an elegiac essay—where the Bible Belt came unbuckled. It was famous for its booze and hookers and transvestites, and for a Mardi Gras where the promise of some raucous cheers and a handful of beads could induce cheerful wardrobe malfunctions on Chartres Street. It was where the Midwest drained out to the sea, where Mark Twain headed from Missouri, and where conventioneers and college kids headed to get drunk and get laid.

As it evolved into a major modern tourist destination fed by air travel, the Crescent City got its inevitable Convention Center and Superdome. Jim Garrison, the district attorney who became notorious for his obsessive investigations into the Kennedy assassination, tried to clean it up. Increasingly, the French Quarter became a theme park on the subject of its own former self. There was stubborn resistance to sanitization and Disneyfication, though, and the wicked old place never really lost its underlying authenticity.

But when the levees broke, it was clearly the wrong place and the wrong time to be poor and black. In New Orleans, as in most large American cities, race, class, and topographic advantage closely correlate. Tourists who flew in and took cabs to their hotels often barely noticed, but New Orleans is the most African-American of all the nation's major cities. It is mostly very poor, and deeply oppressed by hopelessness, drugs, and violent crime. The most desperate areas, such as the Ninth Ward, are generally low-lying, while the more affluent inhabitants are housed on the higher, better-drained, and breezier ground. When the floodwaters poured in, the aerial photographs looked like GIS plots of income levels.

Not only that, the poorest of its citizens were the least equipped to deal with disaster. In a city that was sparsely served by public transportation, many didn't have cars in which to flee. They didn't have money for gasoline or fares. They didn't have computers to surf into the Web to find out what was going on, or credit cards for hotel rooms, or concerned and resourceful out-of-town relatives to look out for them. Many were uneducated, isolated, and immobilized by health problems. They had little choice—tragically, as it turned out—but to stay and try to see it through.

Now that the initial crisis has passed, the long, slow, sad process of drainage and cleanup will continue. So will the angry recriminations about the Bush Administration's shameful failure to prepare adequately and respond swiftly to a catastrophe that everyone knew was coming. America will struggle to absorb the lessons of the circle of hell that the Superdome became. And the debate will begin about what to do next.

Will New Orleans simply be bulldozed, as one prominent politician has already suggested? Will it become the Atlantis of our time—a storied city lost beneath the water? This seems unlikely. Cities may decline and fade away when they run out of essential resources or political, economic, and cultural luck, but cities that had otherwise been reasonably functional are rarely erased by sudden natural disasters or wartime destruction—no matter how terrible. Between 1100 and 1800, for example, Baghdad, Moscow, Aleppo, Mexico City, and Budapest all lost more than half of their populations owing to wars, but were successfully rebuilt. London, Atlanta and Chicago survived their great fires, and Lisbon, San Francisco, Tokyo, Mexico City, and Tangshan their great earthquakes. Darwin and Chittagong came back after immensely destructive storms. Even after the most brutal attempts to obliterate them by modern technological means, Warsaw, Coventry, Dresden, Hiroshima, and Nagasaki are still there.

There have been exceptions, but not many. Pompeii never came back, but this was a case in which there were no survivors to return, and the site was completely buried by lava and ash. The same was true of St. Pierre, Martinique, which was totally and permanently destroyed by the eruption of Mount Pelée in 1902.

In part, cities get rebuilt because they serve important functions in larger regional, national, and global systems, and this generates pressure to get them up and running again to fill the gap. In part, as well, it is because the value of a city's site is rarely destroyed completely by a traumatic event. And, in part, it is because the displaced survivors grieve for their lost home (in Marc Fried's famous phrase) and desperately want to recreate it by returning to the same place. Rebuilding, on that precise spot, becomes an act of redemption. The obvious vulnerability of a sunken patch of land between the levees of the Mississippi and Lake Pontchartrain, smack in the path of regular hurricanes off the Gulf of Mexico, will not deter this.

The simplest strategy for physical reconstruction is to approximate what was there before. The literal recreation of a lost home has an undeniable emotional appeal, and it minimizes both intellectual effort and political difficulty. Ambulance-chasing developers and contractors like it because they see it as a way of swiftly getting their hands on reconstruction funds. But this would also regenerate the pathologies that have so burdened New Orleans in the past. It would be bolder and better to set the goal of making the city a better place.

Imagine, for a moment, what could be done. The Crescent City could be rebuilt as a model of sophisticated, responsible, coastline management and flood control infrastructure—a source of inspiration for the many other coastal cities that are threatened by global warming and rising sea levels. It could equalize opportunity and risk by transforming the old, deeply discriminatory geography of race and class. It could disdain postcard historicism and sentimental self-parody for the tourists—boldly celebrating, instead, an authentic, vital, continually innovating and evolving mash-up of cultures.

The scenes of bodies floating in the toxic flood were as inevitable as the climax of a Greek tragedy. They resulted from more than a century of hubris in the face of nature, neglect, and indifference to the plight of the poor. But there is now a chance to set a new direction. New Orleans, after Katrina, could be the right place and the right time to begin building a great twenty-first-century city.

13

BEST PRACTICES

A recent survey concluded that the world's most influential brands were Starbucks, Ikea, Apple, Google, and al-Jazeera. Fair enough, but I'm surprised that God didn't make the top five. He has been marketed globally for just about ever. Like Calvin Klein, he's an international household word.

Product placement strategies have been particularly effective for the deity. His representatives have succeeded, in the American market, with placements in the Declaration of Independence ("Laws of Nature and of Nature's God"), on banknotes ("In God we trust"), in the Pledge of Allegiance ("One Nation under God"), and in swearing to tell the truth in court ("So help me God").

The account has made use of some top writers, and they have come up with some great slogans. "God for Harry, England, and Saint George!" for example, ranks right up there with "Finger lickin' good," "Pepsi generation," and "Don't leave home without it."

As Cecil B. DeMille demonstrated, nationwide outdoor advertising also helps to get the word out. To publicize the opening of his 1956 Paramount epic *The Ten Commandments* (the one that has Anne Baxter's

Nefertiti cooing to Charlton Heston's Moses: "You can worship any God you like as long as I can worship you") he had hundreds of Ten Commandments monuments fabricated in granite and installed outside America's city halls. His stars went on the road, sponsored by the Fraternal Order of Eagles, to unveil them. His art director dreamed up their now-familiar boogie board shape. It made a great image. Who can forget the sight of the bronzed Heston striding down from Mount Sinai, with a tablet under his arm, *Baywatch* style, like he's about to surf the Red Sea?

The old huckster DeMille was, I suppose, simply going for boffo at the box office. But his site-specific installations had the effect, through the juxtaposition of synecdoches—fragments standing for greater wholes—of architecturally announcing the unity of God and government. That's fine if, like Osama bin Laden, you're a fan of theocracies. But it bothered the American Civil Liberties Union and the Americans United for Separation of Church and State, and they eventually began to sue. As a result, city councils hastily removed tablets from civic settings in Milwaukee, Duluth, Salt Lake City, Provo, Kansas City, and many other places. These rejectamenta were often reinstalled at locations suitably distant, reversing the symbolism through ritual enactment of the *separation* of civic and religious realms. In Manhattan, Kansas, for example, the local DeMille tablet got carted off to the Heritage Court Entrance of Manhattan Christian College.

Sensing a PR disaster that even the slickest reputation management consultants couldn't contain, the city of Casper, Wyoming, got rid of its tablet in a particularly big hurry when an organization called God Hates Fags started agitating for a companion monument inscribed: "Thou shalt not lie with mankind as with womankind; it is abomination."

In Montgomery, the newly elected chief justice, Roy Moore, pulled off a publicity stunt that DeMille himself might have envied by bringing in a crane and plunking down a late-Brando-sized, 5,280-pound version in the rotunda of the state courthouse. It looked a bit like a granite washing machine with tattoos. For many Alabamans, Moore's theatrics evoked stirring memories of George Wallace standing defiantly at the Birmingham schoolhouse door. They rallied around Roy's Rock. Moore was swiftly tossed out of office by his understandably horrified fellow judges, and his stone stooge was shipped back to the Clark Memorials warehouse. But it had made him—well, I have to say it—a rock star of the religious right. It's now on tour on a flatbed truck, and Moore is running for governor.

All this commotion isn't about *what* the Ten Commandments say, but about *where* it's said. It's about the symbolism of spatial association, not the literary content itself. That's probably just as well, since the Ten Commandments actually aren't very good copy. They could have used an editor. For one thing, there are too many of them to fit as bullet points on a PowerPoint slide, and the message gets fuzzy. As someone once remarked (I think it was Bertrand Russell, and if not it should have been), they are like an exam question. You need only attempt six out of ten.

The first few are just legal boilerplate—exclusivity, artwork, name in vain, and holidays. Then we're told to honor our parents, which seems reasonable enough, though a bit off message. Finally, it's down to the serious business: killing, stealing, lying, fornicating, and coveting. But the presentation, in ye olde English diction and faux-Egyptian format, just doesn't grab the reader's attention.

Pinpoint marketing would be far more effective. To celebrate the fiftieth anniversary of DeMille's classic, God's prohibitions could be posted, like the health warnings on cigarette packets, at the precise sites of potential transgressions. "Don't covet," for example, might work well on magazine advertisements, billboards, shop window displays, and other incitements to desire and possession. "Don't commit adultery" could be printed on hotel room key cards. It's too late to inscribe "Don't steal" in the lobby of Enron's headquarters, but there are plenty of other corporate office towers awaiting suitable treatment, and maybe the Fraternal Order of Eagles could work on it. Killing: let's start with gun shops, Texas death row prisons, and weapons laboratories.

13

As for bearing false witness, it's probably best to concentrate on the untruths uttered by political leaders, since these do the most harm. It would be useful, perhaps, to inscribe "Don't lie" over the doors of the White House and Number 10 Downing Street, but that might be thought disrespectful. Better to save it for those famous stockpiles of WMDs when they are uncovered by our victorious forces in Iraq.

14

MAMA DON'T TAKE MY MEGAPIXELS

"I got a Nikon camera, I love to take a photograph, so Mama, don't take my Kodachrome away."

Well, in the end, Paul Simon's Mama had no say in the matter. Technological evolution has taken our Kodachrome away.

You could see this moment coming for years. Still, it was a shock. Recently, Nikon announced that it would stop making most of its 35-millimeter film cameras in order to concentrate on digital models. Konica Minolta quickly followed with an announcement that it was withdrawing from the camera and color film business. Meanwhile, Kodak has sharply cut back production of its famous color film, and is reducing the number of processing laboratories. We are witnessing the end of a technological subculture that has flourished since the 1930s, and has simultaneously supported and shaped the visual discourse within which architects form, fix, and exchange their ideas.

This subculture had its ancestry in the technologies of the illustrated printed book. Before these emerged, as André Malraux pointed out in *Museum Without Walls*, even the most curious and persistent of artists and architects could only make themselves familiar with a tiny fraction of the many works, scattered around the world, that might otherwise engage their interest. Furthermore, in the absence of good visual records, efforts to compare and classify widely separated works could only rely upon imperfect memory. Palladio's *Four Books of Architecture*, and the many illustrated treatises that followed, remedied this situation be presenting extensive, classified collections in compact format. Flipping pages could now replace actual travel from site to site—though Inigo Jones still found it worthwhile to brave the brigands and go to see Palladio's works for himself.

These published drawings reduced architectural works to the draftsmen's conceptions of their essences—much as printed musical scores abstract away from the complexities and imperfections of actual performances. This was consistent with the classical distinction between essential and accidental properties of things, and it allowed varied interpretation, both in the imaginations of readers and in the works of imitators. Lord Burlington at Chiswick, and Thomas Jefferson at Monticello, were able to study the plates and then produce their own, highly personal versions of Palladio.

With the invention of chemical photography in the 1830s, and its immediate alliance with international travel and communication networks, the character of the discourse began to shift. "Space and time have ceased to exist," Théophile Gautier announced in 1858. In a rhapsodic tone anticipating that of more recent media gurus, he elaborated: "The locomotive pants and grinds in a whirlwind of speed . . . the electric fluid has taken to carrying the mail . . . the daguerreotype opens its brass-lidded eye of glass, and a view, a ruin, a group of people, is captured in an instant."

Unlike plan and section drawings, instantaneous, high-resolution black-and-white photographs recorded buildings at particular moments, under particular lighting conditions, from particular viewpoints. They emphasized fine detail, nuances of tonality, and the effects of wear and weather. Gradually, they transformed a discourse of essences into one that was much more pungently spiced with contingent particularity—

well suited to a taste for the romantic and picturesque. John Ruskin gushed of some daguerreotypes that he had purchased in Venice in 1845, as he certainly wouldn't of Palladio's austere plates: "Every chip of stone and stain is there."

When John Soane lectured at the Royal Academy, before photographs were available, he had relied upon the hundreds of large display drawings that are still preserved in the Soane Museum. When daguerreotypes and photographic prints first appeared, they weren't of much help in the lecture hall, since they were far too small for mass viewing. This problem was solved in 1850, with the invention of the glass lantern slide. In the following decades, historians of art and architecture took it up, and began to develop the practices of the slide lecture.

By the early years of the twentieth century, Heinrich Wölfflin—a great proponent of comparisons and contrasts—was giving double-screen slide lectures in Berlin. This established a dominant genre, within which the tendentious pairing functioned as an indispensable rhetorical device. As the century neared its end, you could always tell the architects and art historians on campus; they were the ones walking around with the emblems of their guild, pairs of slide carousels, under their arms.

As the conventions of the slide lecture evolved, color gradually supplanted black-and-white. Some early lantern slides were hand-tinted. Agfa introduced color lantern slides in the 1920s, and smaller-format 35-millimeter Kodachrome slides appeared in 1936. They soon permeated architecture's darkened lecture halls with those nice bright colors, those greens of summers. In the virtual world that Kodachrome constructed, it was always a sunny day.

To support slide presentations, architectural schools and offices built up impressive slide libraries—some containing hundreds of thousands of images. These collections (particularly the ones located at influential schools) implicitly defined the architectural canon, and served as loci for practices of organizing and transmitting it. Owing to the simple fact that a slide could only be in one place at a time, the classification systems that organized physical storage in drawers—no matter how ideologically questionable and outdated—became powerful, unavoidable conceptual frameworks. Traveling scholars returned with their slides, like hunters with their trophies, to add to these organized accumulations. Copy stands enabled semilegal appropriation of images from books. Large light tables, like film editing suites, became crucibles of creative recombination—places to prepare visual narratives by sorting, sequencing, and arranging in pairs. In the hands of masters like Vincent Scully at Yale, slide-accompanied verbal performances became unforgettable theater. And, to make sure that students paid attention and got it, there were slide quizzes.

Slide culture reached its peak in the 1970s through to the 1990s, when the technology had become highly sophisticated and widely distributed, but had not yet been challenged by digital imaging. In the historicizing postmodernism that appeared and then disappeared during this period, slide imagery rebounded into space. Charles W. Moore, its most erudite, witty, and influential exponent, traveled endlessly, was never without his Nikon, and amassed a vast personal slide collection from which he drew continually in his work. His most famous projects, like the Piazza d'Italia in New Orleans and the Moore House in Austin, were eclectic collages of remembered motifs and found objects in exuberant, Kodachrome colors. They are best seen under blue skies.

Soon, though, slides will be made no more. The great slide libraries are already giving way to online digital image collections, and slide-drawer retrieval operations to downloading. Metadata and search engines, not traditional classification schemes, structure the new visual discourse. Google's page ranking algorithm establishes the new canon; you're in it if you attract enough links. Presentations are prepared and edited on laptop computers, using cut-and-paste software instead of light-tables. Video projectors have driven slide carousels from classrooms and lecture halls. If you can't find an image you need, you just do a Google Image search, download whatever this turns up, and paste it into your presentation.

Mama, don't take my PowerPoint away.

15

INSTRUMENTS AND ALGORITHMS

Drawing with a free hand is like dancing on paper. It can be as energetic as crunk, or a more sedate and reflective activity like (in the words of Paul Klee) taking a line for a walk. The result, in any case, is a trace of improvised motion. Lines have attack and decay. At each point they register the momentary direction, speed, pressure, and angle of a marker engaging a surface, and their numerous, subtle variations carry meaning.

Making a freehand drawing is a performance, and it helps if you have a skilled performer's repertoire of practiced moves. The performance may be private and silent, like solitary prayer. It may be part of a dialogue, as when a critic picks up a pencil to explain an idea to a student. It may even be public and highly theatrical, as when a professor declaims to a packed auditorium while sketching on a blackboard. But whatever the circumstances of the performance, it is impossible to repeat exactly. For those who were present at the unique enactment, the complex marks that remain trigger memories of a context, a subject, and perhaps a conversation.

Producing a drawing with instruments is an altogether more disciplined, modularized, replicable activity. The task is always broken down into discrete, standardized steps executed with mechanical devices. Most commonly, these are steps of tracing lines with straightedges and arcs with compasses, but there are also instruments for production of ellipses, parabolas, and so on. The resulting marks are not to be read as records of an artist's hand in motion, but as symbols standing for timeless Platonic abstractions. Accidents and imperfections of execution, then, are just meaningless blemishes.

Euclid's beautiful constructions are specified sequences of these elementary operations. To erect a perpendicular bisector on a given straight line, for example, you must: (1) strike an arc from one end of the line; (2) keeping the radius constant, strike an arc from the other end; (3) construct a straight line through the two intersection points of the arcs. Once you know Euclid's constructions, you can form perpendiculars, parallels, and other well-defined relationships of lines and arcs, and you can build up more complex figures, such as equilateral triangles, squares, rectangles, and trapezoids. Using the same means, you can then assemble these figures into still larger compositions, and so on recursively. In other words, elementary drafting instruments, together with Euclid's constructions, rigorously define a graphic vocabulary and syntax.

If you want to tell a draftsperson how to produce a particular drawing, you can specify the necessary sequence of discrete, standard operations. Any competent draftsperson should be able to execute the sequence to produce exactly the same result. The sequence is, then, what we now call an algorithm.

It is not always necessary to specify the steps explicitly, at the most elementary level. If you are confident that your draftsperson knows how to construct a perpendicular bisector, for example, you can simply give that higher-level instruction. This corresponds to the powerful computer programming idea of abstraction, which is provided for in programming languages by means of constructs such as procedures, functions, and objects.

In drafting instruments, useful abstractions may similarly be embodied in the mechanics of specialized devices. Tee-squares and parallel rules, for example, enable the quick construction of parallels, and wooden or plastic triangles enable the addition of perpendiculars. If you carefully examine a set of drafting instruments, you can discover not only the graphic vocabulary and syntax that they imply, but also some of the abstractions that structure practical graphic construction processes.

When computer graphics technology emerged in the 1960s, the most fundamental idea underlying it was that a straight line, an arc, or any other sort of curve could be described as the trace of a point moving across a surface or through space. The shape of the curve could be described parametrically—by means of formulas that expressed coordinates as functions of time. Procedures containing these formulas became the computer graphics equivalents of straightedges, compasses, and French curves. Higher-level procedures, which were built from these, implemented Euclid's constructions. The instructions for production of complete drawings could be encoded as sequences of calls, with appropriate parameters, to the available procedures. These sequences could be executed repeatedly, and even carried out on different computers, to produce exactly the same results. Dematerialized software, rather than wood and metal instruments, now operated on the graphic construction. A computer, instead of a draftsperson, executed the algorithms.

The idiosyncrasies of the artist's hand were thus completely eliminated from the process. Drawings could be specified by typing in commands and numbers, or by pointing and clicking with a mouse and a cursor. You could even use a speech interface, if you wanted, to talk a drawing into existence. It didn't matter, so long as the necessary symbols got into the data structure—a reduction of the drawing to its Platonic essence.

Since then, computer graphics and computer-aided design systems have enormously extended their ranges of graphic primitives and higher-level procedures. Relying upon software skills rather than mechanical ingenuity, graphics programmers first replicated the functions of traditional drafting instruments, and then went far beyond them. This has made a wider graphic vocabulary available to designers, together with a more elaborate syntax—in all, a richer and potentially more expressive graphic and spatial language.

In particular, complex curves have become as commonplace, and are now nearly as simple for a designer to manipulate, as straight lines and arcs. And software tools combined with dynamic displays now allow designers to think of lines, shapes, surfaces, architectural elements, and even complete buildings as elastic objects that can be tweaked and twisted endlessly on the screen. These are no longer, as in the era of physical instruments and paper, things that are frozen and rigid on the page. Final designs, then, are like frames selected from scenes of ongoing motion and transformation. The buildings that result are actually as rigid, static, and rooted in the ground as those that were drawn on paper, but sometimes—as in the projects of Zaha Hadid, for example—they manage to allude to their origins in the more fluid, dynamic space of the computer screen.

Something has, of course, been lost. Fine drawing instruments are wonderfully crafted, beautiful things. They feel good in the hand, and there is a particular satisfaction—which older architects can still recall—in their swift and skilled use. But, for those with eyes to see, there is something to take their place. The code of an elegantly constructed graphics algorithm has an austere, functional beauty that can take your breath away. Perhaps, one day, the Building Museum will nostalgically exhibit the software tools of yesteryear.

16

THEORY OF BLACK HOLES

Inmate jurisprudence at Guantánamo Bay is not complex. Roach Motel's famous old slogan says it all. They check in but they don't check out.

Gitmo is hardly unusual, though. It is not, as Tony Blair would have it, "an anomaly," but merely the latest example of something that shows up whenever rulers get desperate. For centuries, they have resorted to black holes—special places where the nation's laws don't apply, and where what happens inside stays there. Of course there have always been "exceptional circumstances" to justify them. Only the enabling technologies of transportation, containment, and suppression of scrutiny have changed.

These are the places where—away from prying eyes and bleeding hearts—the power of the state most ruthlessly confronts the vulnerability of the body. These are the architectural enablers of the ancient practices of degradation, abuse, torture, and execution. They provide the necessary facilities, they equip political leaders with deniability, and they allow the public the comfort of seeing and hearing no evil.

The primitive prototype was the Tower of London—the forbidding urban fortress that not only enforced state authority but also expressed its presence. The tower had its heyday as a place of state-sponsored bodily harm in the sixteenth and seventeenth centuries, when the life-and-death political struggle between Catholics and Protestants seemed to justify every means of squeezing out information about threats and plots. As Francis Bacon crisply put it: "In the highest cases of treasons, torture is used for discovery, and not for evidence." The trouble, of course, is that such places can become hated symbols of the sins of the regime, and potential sites of protest. Look what happened to the Bastille.

Furthermore, urban prisons don't scale. By the eighteenth century, the growing accumulation of incarcerated men, women, and children had created a refuse disposal problem for Georgian London. For a while, the Thames seemed the solution. It was a place to dump sewage and toss trash, and also to contain convicts in crowded, rotting hulks. Then—just as New York's garbage barges now transport the city's solid waste to distant landfills—London took to transporting its criminal class to Australia. This utilized the global sea networks that had been enabled by sail and navigation technology; it exploited the opportunities of empire; and it provided a more efficient, decentralized system of urban hygiene.

Inevitably, the system sucked in political dissidents along with the thieves and prostitutes. The magistrates weren't too fussy about the distinction. "Transportation," as Robert Hughes observed in *The Fatal Shore*, "got rid of the dissenter without making a hero of him on the scaffold. He slipped off the map into a distant limbo, where his voice fell dead at his feet." If you owned a copy of Tom Paine's *Rights of Man*, glorified Jacobinism, or belonged to the Irish Defenders, you stood a good chance of taking a long sea voyage. Not to be outdone, the French soon established their own Devil's Island, and used it for the likes of Captain Dreyfus.

This innovative human disposal system quickly grew into an archipelago of scattered settlements connected by a sea network. Convicts who made trouble in Sydney could be sent on to worse places—Port Arthur in Van Diemen's Land and Kingston on Norfolk Island. Containment was simple; there was nowhere for escapees to go. Flogging was the standard means of additional punishment and the favored enhanced interrogation technique to extract intelligence from reluctant sources. Hangings were commonplace. The jailers had absolute authority, and the long voyage to London assured that very little potentially embarrassing news flowed back to the colonial capital. To be transported was to be consigned—usually forever—to an unknowable, terrifying blank on the map.

In the twentieth century, as nobody can forget, Nazi Germany appropriated this form but updated the technology for its own unspeakable purposes—creating a system of wire-enclosed camps linked by a railway network. The sites were located well away from major urban centers, and media censorship kept the flow of information about them to a minimum—allowing many, later, to say that they just didn't know what their leaders were up to. Anyway, the German newspapers weren't sending out any investigative reporters.

The Soviet Union enthusiastically took up the idea as well, creating a system that Aleksandr Solzhenitsyn was to name the Gulag Archipelago. He entitled one of the chapters in his great, angry book "The History of Our Sewage Disposal System," and he provided a map showing its coast-to-coast extension from Murmansk to Vladivostok. Some existing buildings, particularly monasteries and tsarist prisons, were repurposed for the task, but the characteristic gulag building form was the primitive, remote barracks. As in Germany, a railway network linked the camps to each other and to the cities.

Solzhenitsyn documented the highly developed technologies and management strategies of the gulag system in detail: the varied techniques of arrest; the Black Marias that took prisoners to the railway stations; the special Stolypin cars for prisoners and their guards; the red trains that went direct to the camps; the hidden loading areas; the transfer prisons; and the destination "islands in the archipelago." Concealment was accomplished through use of unmarked vehicles with unspecified destinations, remoteness, and censorship. Solzhenitsyn's book eventually

16

removed the cloak of invisibility and confronted his fellow Soviet citizens with the state within a state, following its own rules, that existed in their midst.

Now, just as an academic exercise, let us imagine how the leaders of a twenty-first century superpower might create a complete system of secret surveillance, seizure of perceived enemies, rendition to distant locations, and disposal without trial into black holes. They would, of course, operate at a global scale and rely upon an air transportation network in place of the sailing ships and steam trains of the past. For concealment, they would employ planes with ambiguous markings that operated from remote corners of airfields. For sites where the law didn't reach, they would begin with military bases on foreign soil. Then, for deeper secrecy they would intimidate and bribe susceptible nations—preferably ones without human rights laws and nosey journalists—to provide clandestine prisons.

To create a facade of legality they would declare the prisoners to be without rights. To preserve a posture of rectitude, they would claim that they didn't condone torture—but define the term so narrowly as to allow most of the vile practices enumerated in the chapter "The Interrogation" of *The Gulag Archipelago.* To discourage opposition, they would deploy a rhetoric of dehumanization, create a climate of fear, and plead the justification of exceptional threat. To make sure that they couldn't be held accountable for what went on, they would make it clear that they didn't want to know.

If citizens didn't ask questions and protest, they would be complicit in evil. But this is all just hypothetical, as the White House press secretary might say. It couldn't actually be happening in our own time, could it? We're more civilized now.

17

ELEGY IN A LANDFILL

She should have died hereafter; there would have been a time for such a word. I'm talking about my hard drive, which recently expired at a particularly inopportune moment.

This set me to dark reflection upon the mortality of the products that globally industrialized society creates and circulates in such prodigious quantities. They strut and fret their hours upon the stage and then are heard no more. And all our yesterdays have lighted things the way to dustbin death. It is a tale, etc. . . . but it does signify something.

As in the natural world, life spans, typical causes of demise, and funerary practices vary from species to species. Buildings, for example, live naturally about as long as giant tortoises and eventually die through loss of their inhabitants. The processes of wear, weathering, corrosion, and ultimate decay into uninhabitable ruin start from the moment of completion and occupancy. It helps to be well constructed to begin with, and physical decline can be slowed through careful maintenance, but it is inexorable. Many buildings, of course, never make it to their allotted spans, and instead expire violently in fires, explosions, earthquakes, or floods; whole neighborhoods of New Orleans, right now, are like battlefields strewn with rotting carcasses. Under conditions of Schumpeterian, creatively destructive capitalism, gangland-style execution becomes the principal cause of building death; when real estate assets outlast their economic usefulness, they are ruthlessly taken out to make way for their successors.

Some deceased buildings, like cremated bodies, leave nothing but heaps of ashes. Others—through the intermediation of junkyards and antique stores—become organ donors. Frequently, the remains just get carted off for burial in landfills. Where they are particularly revered, architectural corpses may be preserved intact, like the embalmed body of Jeremy Bentham in its glass case, for viewing by posterity. In any case, the remains serve as reminders of past eras.

Today's automobiles have roughly the life spans of dogs. If they don't get killed off in crashes, they finally wear out. Mechanical death is generally a process of increasingly frequent failures, leading at last to a merciful decision not to revive. The growing cost of end-of-life car care eventually exceeds the benefit of keeping a vehicle running, so it's economically rational to dispose of it and get a replacement. *Lion King*, circle of life: the next one is always waiting at the dealer's lot.

Income levels determine automotive funerary customs. In affluent communities, tow trucks haul dead cars off to their final resting places on the edge of town. There they are exposed to scavengers for a decent while, and then—safely out of sight of those who loved them—crushed into cubes of scrap steel. In the most desperate areas of inner city or rural poverty, though, nobody can afford to take them away, so they simply remain where they stopped moving. The appearance of rusting car carcasses in a neighborhood is, as everyone knows, a pretty clear symptom of economic distress.

Computers live no longer than hamsters. They are congenitally predisposed to sudden electronic death syndrome resulting from fried processors, disks, or power supplies. But that's not the half of it. As they grow older, our faithful, keyboarded companions crash with increasing frequency and start to lose it—finally becoming incapable of running the latest versions of Microsoft Office. They stop responding to our commands. In the end, despite the protestations of the pro-computer-lifers, we have no choice but to pull their plugs.

Fortunately, in the aftermath of this, there are the consolations of faith. Believing, practicing users hold that computers have immortal files, which, if they haven't been corrupted, ascend to backup. One jubilant day, through appropriate ritual, they will be reincarnated on new hardware.

The lives of mobile phones are nasty, brutish, and short. Some die from trauma when they are dropped. Some fall into toilets and drown. Some get sat on. Some are lost or abandoned and die alone when there's nobody around to recharge their batteries. Some expire tragically in the brief flower of their youth—like the consumptive heroines of romantic novels—from electronic organ failure. Those few that somehow make it to old age grow burdensome, and face the prospect of cold-blooded disembowelment at the hands of their fickle owners—who just open them up and rip out their SIM cards for transfer to newer, flashier models. The victims of serial phone killers are often buried, side-by-side with their predecessors, in dusty desk drawers.

Sooner or later, all gadgets great and small, all appliances, all stained and sagging mattresses, all broken items of furniture, and all emptied packages end up in the garbage. They are tossed out—removed from their privileged places of use and value to grim locations that signify the end. They are conveyed to trashcans, recycling bins, dumpsters, or those transparent plastic bags hanging from metal rings that you find in the streets of Paris. Here they briefly remain, in a kind of purgatory (whence, occasionally, they are retrieved and saved by trash pickers), until T-shirted Charons ferry them away in trucks.

Acts of separation from possessions we no longer want are more crucial to us than they might seem. A world without product death and disposal would be stultifying; we *need* to get rid of things. In one of his slyly perceptive essays (*La Poubelle Agréée*), Italo Calvino observed that throwing away is a psychologically necessary rite of purification and renewal. It is "the first and indispensable condition of being, since one is what one does not throw away." Taking out the trash is a way of discreetly affirming that, for one more day, you have been a producer of detritus and not yet detritus to be carried out yourself.

Minimalist design gestures of taking out the unnecessary flourishes, editorial gestures of taking out the adverbs, and political gestures of taking out the dissidents serve similar psychic purpose. But anal retentives, pack rats, misers, dogmatic architectural preservationists, inhabitants of cities experiencing garbage strikes, writers without editors, and characters like Miss Havisham hoard their stuff and end up losing themselves in it. We define ourselves not only by what we accumulate, but also by what we choose to discard.

For products, it seems, the paths of glory lead but to the landfill. If you're in an elegiac mood at the knell of parting day, you might care to contemplate the endless enactment of advanced capitalism's complementary rituals. Our cities serve simultaneously as sites for desiring, acquiring, and accumulating things, and equally necessarily, as places for ritually separating ourselves from them.

18

THEORY OF EVERYTHING

Like String Theory, the Bag of Chips Theory sets out to explain everything. (I'm talking about the food products alternatively known as crisps, not those referred to in North America as French or freedom fries.) Rigorously pursued, it tells you whatever you need to know about advanced architectural form.

I found that it was easy to become a leading exponent. I just went to my local Star Market and loaded up a cart with every sort of chip I could find. (Think of Charles Darwin collecting Galapagos finches.) To facilitate my studies, I tossed in some guacamole, some clam dip, and a couple of six-packs of Bud Lite.

My experiments (which you may care to replicate—keeping in mind that your local brand names may vary) began with Pringles. The potato-derived synthetic material of these classic chips is extremely fragile, so it must be precisely engineered to achieve structural integrity. Each Pringle takes a standard, double-curved saddle shape that becomes a neat lozenge in plan. It looks like it might be a hyperbolic paraboloid, but this is difficult to confirm without precise laboratory measurements.

Pringles stack nicely, like Eames molded plastic chairs, and they ship in cardboard tubes.

This is all very mid-last-century modernist—wonder material, modularity, repetition, structural expression. Late at night in a hotel room, Pringles from the minibar can give you Proustian moments. Munch one with a beer and it becomes a madeleine—evoking faded memories of, say, Felix Candela's concrete shell restaurant roof in Xochimilco, or Eduardo Catalano's plywood-roofed house in Raleigh.

Ruffles are typologically similar. For their structural performance, though, they rely not only upon curvature, but also upon a secondary system of corrugations. This provides strength in bending, and makes them particularly good for scooping up and retaining dip—an advantage of striation over smoothness that, I believe, went unnoticed by Deleuze and Guattari.

Corn chips (sometimes known as tortilla chips or taco chips) also originate as machine-made regular shapes—triangles, squares, rectangles, and circles. During cooking they develop unevenly distributed stresses that twist them out of the plane—much as you can give a slight twist to a sheet of paper held in your hands. The edges become elegant spline curves, with ruled surfaces in between. In effect, the process randomly tweaks parameters. Consequently, a bag of corn chips does not consist of identical shapes like a tube of Pringles, but of parametric variations on the theme of the ur-chip. This is nonstandard serialism. Deep-frying and oven baking, it seems, are powerful generative procedures in the service of this formal strategy, and opening up a bag of the crunchy results is quicker and cheaper than doing 3-D prints from the output of Rhino or Catia models.

The most overtly architectural chips that I have encountered are the large, thin, fresh tortilla chips that come with takeout from the Forest Café, my local Oaxaca-style restaurant and late-night drinking hole. These have varied, hand-cut shapes, and they twist with a vivacity that you don't find in bagged varieties. They are great for doing Gehry knock-offs. By embedding them in blobs of refried beans you can produce endless riffs on the themes of the Bilbao Guggenheim, the Disney Concert Hall, and the thin, flyaway curved surfaces of the Bard College Auditorium and the Millennium Park Bandshell.

Cheetos and Pirate's Booty (with aged white cheddar) may not, strictly speaking, be chips—indeed, they are so synthetic it isn't clear *what* they are—but it seems to me that they have contributed crucially to chipology. Certainly, they have served to problematize its boundaries. Like popcorn, they appear to be formed by the explosive expansion of some sort of starch, and they take doubly curved, convex forms. With some ingenuity, you can stuff program into scaled-up versions of them, and they have enviable sculptural energy and gestural freshness. They do, however, need to be rationalized for large-scale fabrication. No problem: they can be laser-scanned, approximated by torus parches or NURBS blobs, and then digitally fabricated.

Finally, Cape Cod chips are thicker, crisper, and more intricately gnarled and warped than their rivals—baroque in a bag. I recommend them as snack-food accompaniment to Gilles Deleuze's *Le Pli* (The Fold), which once impressed theorists by interpreting the world as a body of infinite folds and surfaces that twist and weave their way through time and space. Events are combinations of signs in motion, subjects are nomadic, and architecture is endlessly in the process of becoming. Looking back to Leibniz and the origins of the calculus, you can create buildings from continuous curves with inflection points instead of Euclidean lines and arcs. Something like that, anyway—it's all so nineties, and hard to remember now.

You can compose these various chip forms just by heaping them up, which is remarkably easy to do, and has the urbanistic virtue of breaking down the scales of large buildings. Alternatively, as in Toyo Ito's recent Taichung Opera House project, you can constrain them to regular, transparent envelopes—much like dropping them into empty goldfish tanks. This produces buildings that are anatomically equivalent to Spongebob Squarepants, with porous, interiors, and elevations formed simply by sectioning their three-dimensional textures.

As ubiquitous products of global capitalism, industrially produced potato and corn chips have increasingly dominated this discourse. But artisanal banana chips, plantain chips, and taro chips have continued to operate at its margins, and in Southeast Asia you find lots of krupuk—multicolored, prawn-flavored tapioca chips. These begin as thin, flat wafers, but when deep-fried they puff up into large, light, gently curved forms suggesting airy, floating roofs for tropical climates. As with the big blue creampuff of the Graz Kunsthaus, the dual durians of Singapore's Esplanade Performance Center, and the noodle steel of the Beijing Olympic Stadium, they valorize resistant practices of culinary regionalism.

Forms grabbed from these varied bags of chips were genuinely fresh and interesting at first, especially when—as with Bilbao—the buildings they generated made sense as urban monuments. But they have since become stale and unappealing. Chip architecture has mostly descended into scale kitsch—the cheap thrill provided by enlarging familiar shapes to surprising size and realizing them in unexpected materials. It has entered the cultural category previously represented by those big red lobsters you see outside seafood restaurants on Cape Cod, and satirized by Jeff Koons's forty-foot, flower-covered "Puppy."

19

DEEP FOCUS

The commanders of George W. Bush's War on Terror have been better at putting feet in their mouths than boots on the ground where they were needed. CIA Director George Tenet remarked that the existence of Iraqi weapons of mass destruction was a "slam dunk." Vice President Dick Cheney insisted that American troops would be "greeted as liberators." General William Boykin failed in his attempts to capture Osama bin Laden, but no problem. "I knew that my God was bigger than his," said the general. "I knew that my God was a real God, and his was an idol."

Now Rear Admiral Harry Harris Jr. has distinguished himself. There were dozens of suicide attempts, and then three simultaneous suicides, on his watch as Guantánamo Bay camp commander, but it couldn't have been the fault of that wretched place. "I believe this was not an act of desperation," he announced, "but an act of asymmetrical warfare waged against us." How would he strike back? Would he order a few Gitmo guards to hang themselves in response?

I have to admit, though, that the admiral is on to something. He has added a useful new trope—let's call it *contortio per asymmetriam*—to the catalogue of those with Greek and Latin names that we have inherited from antiquity. The trick is to deny that a thing is what it plainly seems to be, insert a "but," and then spin it as its opposite by means of pseudotechnical modifiers. For example, all those things Mr. Bush and Mr. Blair told us about Saddam Hussein's weapons of mass destruction and al-Qaeda links weren't lies, but afactual speech acts directed against obstructionists. Proclaiming "mission accomplished" onboard an aircraft carrier May Day 2003 wasn't a vainglorious absurdity, but was prospectively asynchronously true.

The rhetorical armory of the War on Terror isn't confined to sound bites. It extends, as well, to the persuasive uses of public space, spectacle, and electronically distributed imagery. The dramaturgy framing "mission accomplished," for example, derived from that of the Roman Triumph—the parade of a victorious commander in chief through the streets of the city—but was shrewdly updated to exploit the spin potential of modern transportation and media technologies. As you may recall, the Roman Triumphator entered the city in a chariot drawn by four horses, and then progressed along the Via Sacra to the Capitol where he offered sacrifice to Jupiter. In the media Triumphus for Iraq, the president flew in a S-3B Viking aircraft to the USS Abraham Lincoln where he announced that major combat operations had ended and asked God to continue to bless America.

Clearly this shipboard spectacle was staged for video cameras, broadcast, and the Internet, which, in any case, provided the only ways for members of the civilian public to see it. Its visual strategies were appropriated directly from Leni Riefenstahl's reinvention for film of the Triumphus (in this case Hitler's arrival in Nuremberg for the 1934 rally) in *Triumph of the Will*—probably the first public event to be planned not only as impressive live action but also to create powerful propaganda footage. Like Dubbya, Hitler hadn't actually *won* any victories in 1934, of course, but facts weren't the point; Riefenstahl's job was to create an unchallengeable *impression* of a powerful, resolute leader who would defend the fatherland against its enemies and restore its honor.

The fuhrer's flack delivered brilliantly; her documentary-style film opened with the leader's dramatic arrival by airplane, and then showed him cheered by uniformed masses. To present him as a hero, she shot close-ups from below as he stared past the camera into the distance—the same technique that Alberto Korda was to employ, with even greater success, in his iconic portrait of Ché Guevara in Havana. To end on a note of religiosity, she used an image on the Nürnberg Frauenkirche. No doubt about it, that figure in photogenic military getup was Top Gun.

Similarly, the Bush Triumphant money shot showed the president from below in center frame, at a podium, with the impressive superstructure of the carrier rising behind him. Hanging from it was a huge "mission accomplished" banner, appearing like a comic-strip speech balloon over his head. (Months later, when it became embarrassingly obvious that the mission was far from accomplished, his spin control apparatus denied that they had put it there and blamed the Navy.) Whoever set this up had learned a crucial lesson from Gregg Toland, the cinematographer of *Citizen Kane*. Toland's innovative "deep focus" framing of scenes placed actors in the foreground and potently evocative objects in the background, making a narrative point through their juxtaposition. Parents bicker in the foreground while, seen through a window, the lonely infant plays with Rosebud; the elderly Kane in his castle broods in close-up as his disaffected trophy wife ignores him on the other side of the room; and, in the film's most memorable image, the deluded demagogue speaks from a podium with an enormous, self-aggrandizing banner at his back.

Sub-Toland deep focus has become a ready-made, failsafe propaganda technique—effective for getting a message out, but since visual juxtaposition isn't really assertion, avoiding the risk of getting caught out in an actual lie. Just set up the possibility and any Fox News cameraman or tabloid photographer will do the rest. It worked so well on the Abraham Lincoln that the Bush wranglers used it again, two years later, when the president flew into the flooded city of New Orleans to announce on television: "We will do what it takes." The floodlit Saint Louis Cathedral appeared as a backdrop, visually assuring us of the speaker's faith-based good intentions. *Ut pictura poesis,* I guess.

Political speech and political staging and framing now work seamlessly together—a point that would not have been lost on George Orwell. It is more than half a century since he published his fierce essay "Politics and the English Language," in which he warned that modern political language was "designed to make lies sound truthful and murder respectable" through use of exhausted idioms, passive voice constructions that obscure responsibility, and ready-made phrases that conceal horrors. He was right, and the strategies that he fingered still play a role. The near-dead metaphors of choice, right now, are archaically nautical—"staying the course" versus "cutting and running" in Iraq—with the original references of these phrases to anchors, sails, and stormy seas long forgotten by the hacks who mouth them. But, as media-savvy operatives have figured out, ready-made visual constructions can be even more effective. An exhausted picture is worth a thousand exhausted words.

20

DAPPLED THINGS

"Glory be to God for dappled things," with its cunningly crafted sequence of vowel sounds, is the line from Gerard Manley Hopkins that everyone remembers. Like many of the great Italian baroque churches, the shaved-down sonnet that it opens is a fervent Jesuit offering of praise.

But pied beauty hasn't much appealed to the architects and theorists of high modernism. They have been happier with simple, hard-edged forms and consistent surfaces. The young Corb did it in white; Mies did it in black; and de Stijl did it in primaries. Even the historicizing postmodernists of the seventies and eighties did it with posterlike cutout shapes and flat colors.

This isn't just an arbitrary formal strategy; it is deeply rooted in techniques of industrial production. These favor discrete, repeating parts that can be prefabricated and later assembled. They depend mostly upon uniform, manufactured materials that behave in predictable, controllable ways. And they treat deviations from the norm not as welcome variation, but as defects and blemishes to be minimized through strict quality control.

Frank Gehry's recently completed IAC office tower, in the West Chelsea neighborhood of Manhattan, breaks with this dogma. The obvious and shocking thing about it is that the windows and spandrels of the curtain wall don't have clearly defined edges. They fade gradually into each other, producing an effect of alternating fuzzy bands running across the facade. During the day, the spandrels are white fuzz, and during the night the windows are light fuzz.

The effect is produced by fritted glass panels with high-density white ceramic dot patterns at the upper and lower edges that gradually diminish toward the middle, and eventually vanish entirely. There is no way to say where the opaque spandrel ends and the transparent window begins. The pattern echoes the halftone screens used by printers, and up-close it recalls graduated Zip-a-tone. Furthermore, the surface isn't flat. The panels are cold-formed into gentle curves, producing further complexities from the resulting oblique views and moving highlights—especially when you approach the building by fast-moving car down the West Side Highway. It looks best against Hopkins's "skies of couple-color as a brinded cow."

Gehry has kept the ceilings as clean and simple as possible, since they are mostly what you see through the glass at night; they need to work as bright backgrounds. The petticoat-style shades and the fuzzily framed views out through the frits are great. But the interior, generally, is not nearly as radical as the exterior. Inside, it's a pretty standard office building for Barry Diller's InterActiveCorp, an Internet-era business empire that includes Ticketmaster, the television shopping network HSN, the online dating service Match.com, and the search engine Ask Jeeves. There are the usual corporate corner offices, cubicle farms, screens on desks, and conference rooms.

This is hardly surprising, since modernism's preference for discrete, uniform things has always extended to space planning as well. Rooms have singular functions. Land uses are segregated and zoned. Hopkins, of course, preferred: "Landscape plotted and pieced—fold, fallow, and plough; and all trades, their gear and tackle and trim." So did Jane

Jacobs. But old modernist habits die hard, and anyway, pied program is messy and inconvenient; Charles Moore once remarked that it hurt your fingers when you tried to indicate it on plan with mat knife and color-coded Zip-a-tone.

Hopkins's polemic didn't stop with spatial patterns, but continued to the moral dimension of: "All things counter, original, spare, strange; whatever is fickle, freckled (who knows how?) with swift, slow; sweet, sour; adazzle, dim." It's not a bad line to memorize at a time when demagogues offer us the "moral clarity" of simplistic distinctions and the consolations of intolerant fundamentalism. But Hopkins's God—the one who could make all these wondrously impure and imperfect things—is bigger than their God. Fundamentalism isn't a return to ancient and immutable truths, but a degenerate mutation of modernism.

I can't share Hopkins's faith, but I'll sign up to his manifesto for freckled surfaces, fuzzy boundaries, combinations, contaminations, and complex commingling. Praise him.

21

MORPHOLOGY OF THE BIOPIC

It's the best of all those architect CDs you can now find on Amazon, with some pretty sensational stuff—the story of a young man's complex and ambivalent relationship with his architect father, messy sexual intrigue in the office, an aging master who ruthlessly manipulates everyone around him. As an exploration of the psychic costs of single-minded ambition, it's hard to beat. It's Ibsen's *Master Builder,* in the 1960 Broadway Theater Archive version, with a bow-tied E. G. Marshall as the *bygmester* Halvard Solness. You won't forget the heart-stopping ending, as Solness's winsome young muse waves her shawl in the air and shrieks: "My—my Master Builder!"

Real-life narratives don't come so neatly packaged, of course, so the directors of biopics must look for ways to fit the facts (or passable approximations to them) into similarly compelling structures. And it helps if you can get Russell Crowe to play the lead, as in *A Beautiful Mind,* and *Cinderella Man.*

Sure, some famous architects have been known to throw telephones, but they generally don't have the screen presence of Australian matinee idols; it's hard to imagine any of them carrying off *Gladiator.* And you can bet that they will want to star as themselves, like Muhammad Ali in *The Greatest.* Not that there's budget for anything else. All things considered, then, filming an architect's biography must be a tough assignment.

Fortunately, it turns out that there's a formula. First, you collect as much fly-on-the-wall footage of design process and client meetings as you can. You visit projects, and get some walk-around and drive-around interviews—avoiding the deadly-boring sit-around wherever possible. You pursue some of the more articulate colleagues, critics, friends, and family members for revelatory vignettes. Then you appropriate some standard form of narrative arc—the sort of underlying, allegedly universal arrangement of events that literary theorists like Vladimir Propp and Roland Barthes used to delight in pointing out—go into the editing room, and mash your material onto it.

The narrative of the determined hero-architect overcoming all obstacles seems to be a particular favorite. Peter Rosen's two films on I. M. Pei, *First Person Singular* and *The Museum on the Mountain,* are straightforward exercises within this format, with Pei's elegance and cosmopolitan charm much on display. Pei has genuine star quality, and the camera likes him, but these films plod. Freida Lee Mock's Oscar-winning *Maya Lin: A Strong Clear Vision* is a lot livelier, with a plot straight from Propp's *Morphology of the Folk Tale*: young hero sets out on a quest, encounters mighty villains, is tested in battle, faces seemingly inevitable defeat, but is finally triumphant. Nathaniel Kahn's *My Architect: A Son's Journey* tells the story of Louis Kahn's artistic development and eventual rise to fame—and gains emotional depth by becoming, as well, the story of a son piecing together a film portrait of his complex and elusive father.

Sydney Pollack's recent *Sketches of Frank Gehry* tweaks the conventions of this emerging genre and gets trickier with narrative layering. You do see plenty of Gehry at work, and revisiting his projects. But it's also a buddy movie, reflecting upon the friendship of the director and his subject. Occasionally, Gehry's analyst pops in to offer commentary. And, most interestingly, like the recent Jane Austen join-the-dots job *Becoming Jane*, it's about the construction of self—showing how Frank Gehry made himself into Frank Gehry.

With this, the possibilities of the architect biopic may be exhausted for a while. Perhaps it's time to move on to quantity surveyors.

22

LITTLE BLUE COUPE

Susie, spark of my life, fire of my cylinders. My sin, my soul. Su. Sie.

There has always been something Lolita-like about Disney's animated heroines, but Susie, the Little Blue Coupe, is truest to the type. Humbert Humbert would instantly have recognized her as a nymphet—and it isn't hard to imagine him lurking in the parking lot to catch a lone lustful glimpse of her, since she appeared (animated by Ollie Johnson) in the same forties-and-fifties America that Hum and Lo traversed in their Dream Blue Melmoth sedan. No buxom-fendered Charlotte Haze-mobile, she had a girlish sky-colored body, glistening lips, a honey-hued ragtop, and flirty windshield eyes—a perfect little beauty. With apparently unfeigned innocence, she stretched and wiggled deliciously. And there was a butterfly flutter to her long eyelashes.

"One day," Sterling Holloway's voiceover tells us, "her flashing grille caught the eye of a neat little man in a brown suit. When he saw Susie, it was love at first sight." Soon, Susie and the man were out driving around small town America—rendered in meticulous, shaded perspective by the great background artist Ralph Hulett. They encountered houses with stoops and front lawns lining suburban streets; it was like cruising through a New Urbanist marketing brochure before New Urbanism was new. There was a Main Street with cozy storefronts and red streetcars; it wasn't too different from the Disneyland Main Street in Anaheim, which Disney's designers were working on right about then. The mise-en-scene included a corner drugstore, a bakery, Wong Fong's Hand Laundry, the deco Rialto movie palace, Miller Motors, Joe's Garage, and Maniac Martin's used car lot—where the aging Susie eventually got dumped before, in a nice noirish touch, starting to hang around outside bars on the meaner streets of town.

"The vacuum of my soul managed to suck in every detail of her bright beauty," another dapper man recalled in the notes for his trial. It was Humbert's first glimpse of Lolita lazing beside the pool in the Haze backyard. After Haze Senior had come to her convenient end, and the older-model European had taken illicit possession of the snub-nosed American lovely with pale-gray vacant eyes and soot-black eyelashes, the two hit the highway. Their route began "with a series of wiggles and whorls," in New England. They dipped down to Dixie, crossed the Midwest and the Southwest, reached California, and finally returned along the Canadian border.

Humbert's jailhouse testament says little about the roads they followed, but they must have driven west along the quarter-century-old Route 66—winding from Chicago to L.A., more than two thousand miles all the way. It went through St. Louie, Joplin, Missouri—and if you're old enough to remember Chuck Berry you know the rest—on to Flagstaff, Arizona (don't forget Winona), Kingman, Barstow, and San Bernardino. This renowned highway had begun as an east-west trucking link, rivaling the railroads. Then it served as the best way from Oklahoma to California during the dustbowl thirties—celebrated as the Mother Road by John Steinbeck in *The Grapes of Wrath*. By the time of Humbert and Lolita's shocking road trip, it had evolved into a tourist route lined with gas stations, diners, and motels.

By the end of the forties, private automobiles and the first long-distance roads had generated, on an almost incomprehensibly vast scale, a new kind of American landscape populated by new building types. In earlier stagecoach, riverboat, and railroad towns, travelers didn't have much choice; they alighted where the transportation networks provided for it. That's where services clustered. Now, though, motorists could stop for gas, food, and lodging wherever they wanted. The establishments that provided roadside services had to compete for driver attention—to become irresistible attractions. Like follies in eighteenth-century gardens, they vied to present the most surprising, eye-catching forms. They traded in local culinary specialties and curios; they advertised nearby landscape wonders and historic sites; and they enthusiastically embraced the exuberant possibilities of neon. Views became packaged products with places to stop and take them in and names that functioned like titles of paintings. On Main Streets, increasingly, drive-up establishments seeking the attention of passers-through jostled for space and visibility with Susie-town walk-up businesses that served local needs.

This summer's Disney animation blockbuster, *Cars*, is a spectacular visual homage to the now-vanished landscape of small-town roadside attractions. This brief efflorescence had gradually begun to fade away about a decade after Humbert and Lolita had ended their travels, when construction of the Interstate Highway System began in 1956. The concrete carriageways of the Interstates don't wind; they slice straight through the landscape from interchange to interchange. They don't thread through Main Streets, but carefully avoid town centers. In place of quirky mom-and-pop businesses strung out along the blacktop, they have standardized franchises lurking at freeway exits. The fictional setting for *Cars* is Radiator Springs, a decaying Western town on Route 66 that had lost all of its traveler business when it was bypassed by Interstate 40.

The characters are 3-D-modeled derivatives of Susie's four-wheeled friends, and the story isn't much—an insipid variant on the smug city slicker discovers small town virtues formula. The hero is Lightning McQueen, an obnoxiously selfish hotshot racing car who falls for a local, finds his inner whatever, and becomes a better automotive product when he accidentally strays from the Interstate and gets stranded in the town the freeways forgot. His love interest is Sally, a little blue Porsche Carrera who has dropped out of the fast-lane life in Los Angeles; she hikes her spoiler to flash a pinstripe tattoo, but as a temptress she's really not in her little blue predecessor's league. The appearance of a dark and grumpy Hudson Hornet does briefly raise hopes of some Nabokovian complexities, but he turns out to have the voice of Paul Newman and a heart of gold.

You quickly figure out that *Cars* is mostly about lovingly re-creating and presenting for our nostalgic pleasure a sunny high-desert landscape dotted with crumbling mid-century buildings—the Cadillac Range and Ornament Valley, the Wheel Well and Cozy Cone motels, Flo's V8 Café, Luigi's Tires, and many more. It asks us to contemplate the contrast between the landscapes of today and those of an idealized past—much as in Pugin's contrasts between the industrial cities of his day and steepled medieval towns, or in the temple-studded golden-past landscapes painted by Claude and Poussin. It's brilliantly done. Here, at their best moments, Pixar's modelers, texture mappers, and shading directors achieve the computer graphics sublime.

If Lolita had lived, she would be celebrating her 70th birthday this year. Perhaps she would have written a best-selling victim memoir, and gone on Oprah to plug it. I like to think she'd be taking the grandkids to see *Cars* at the multiplex near her retirement community and boring them with reminiscences of the days before the Interstates.

23

BICYCLE SOCIALISM

You can almost hear a chorus of old hippies smugly singing "Age of Aquarius." Nicolas Sarkozy's France seems an unlikely place for a triumph of tribal love-rock communalism, but there it is. Or so it seems. In Paris, since just after Bastille Day this summer, free bicycles have been everywhere.

Even more surprisingly, the sudden *bicyclette* invasion turns out to be all about advertising—the result of a deal between the mayor of Paris, Bertrand Delanoë, and the billboard company JC Decaux. Under it, JC Decaux provides and maintains the bicycles, and in return gains control of the city's outdoor advertising space. The business model is derived from that of Google, which provides a free search service, and then happily pockets the profits from the opportunity that this affords to place advertisements in front of user eyeballs. JC Decaux has simply transferred it from cyberspace to urban space, substituting provision of bicycle access to the City of Lights for user access to the City of Bits, and replacing on-screen banner-ads with billboards.

Actually, the distinctive grey *Vélib*, as the bikes have been branded, are free only for the first half hour. After that, the cost per hour rises to approximately that of riding the Métro, and eventually to a punitive level. It is a carefully calibrated pricing system, designed to encourage short-term use.

Hundreds of electronic Vélib racks have been distributed throughout the city, dramatically transforming many streetscapes. This extends a familiar game for JC Decaux, which has long been in the business of providing bus shelters and other street furniture—which, of course, carry advertising.

To rent a bike from one of these new racks, you swipe your access card to identify yourself and set the meter running. This unhooks a bicycle, and it is then yours to ride—and to take responsibility for, until you deposit it in another rack. Since the Vélib system tracks renters in this way, it has an effective defense against misuse, vandalism, and theft. Sadly but realistically, this electronic management scheme projects a much dimmer view of human nature than that of the pioneering bicycle sharing schemes of the sixties, in Amsterdam and elsewhere. These relied upon trust, with the consequence that all their machines were stolen, trashed, and tossed into canals with legendary swiftness.

Unlike rental cars, Vélib bicycles do not have to be taken back to the racks where they were picked up. In other words, this is a one-way rental system. In dense, mixed-use urban environments, where trips are more-or-less randomly distributed, such systems turn out to be effectively self-organizing. If they are carefully managed, they do not often leave racks empty where there is demand for bikes, or jammed full where riders want to return them. When self-organization does occasionally fail—for example, at the bottom of the hill in Montmartre where there are often too many bicycles, and at the top of the hill where there are not enough, JC Decaux just sends around workers with trucks to retrieve bikes from over-supplied racks and drop them off at under-supplied ones.

After just a few months, the liberating, equalizing, fraternity-inducing free bicycle is already deeply embedded in Parisian culture. The racks have begun to function, in their neighborhoods, as social magnets—new village wells. This brings romance, or at least, new flirtation opportunities and pick-up lines. We can surely expect a film with winsome young stars that will do for the Vélib what *Roman Holiday* did for the Vespa.

Furthermore (a sure sign of its smashing success) this new mobility system has inspired vigorous though confused ideological debate. The Right thinks that it might be a Socialist plot—probably contrived to get the mayor re-elected, but can't help admiring its entrepreneurial audacity. The Left recognizes it as *their* old idea brought to fruition, but resents its appropriation by big business, and grumbles about the gentrification that it encourages and flaunts—all those affluent, fashionably dressed youngsters speeding around former working-class streets and acting as if they owned them. Don't expect to hear much of this in the cafés of the Left Bank, though: look for the Vélophile and Vélophobe blogs.

But there are no free lunches, and we should not expect bicycles to be any different. The price that Paris must pay is now becoming evident, as an invasion of electronic advertising on bus shelters and street kiosks inexorably follows the wave of bikes. Just as with newspapers, commercial television, and Google, advertising revenue ultimately has to pay the bills. The full extent of the additional advertising that will result, its quality and intrusiveness, and its effect on public space all remain to be seen. It is an open question whether Mayor Delanoé has made a good deal or a Faustian bargain.

Other mayors should watch the outcome carefully, and be prepared to drive hard bargains. If they have not done so already, JC Decaux and their American rival Clear Channel will soon be knocking on their doors. Next is hilly San Francisco: the mayor is running for re-election on a promise of reducing congestion and pollution, and the *Chronicle* reports that the city's board of supervisors is about to vote on a contract with Clear Channel.

24

FAUX BOOK

Obviously enough, the physical packaging of a text shapes its distribution possibilities; printed newspapers will be read in different places, at different times, under different conditions, from email on Blackberries. Less obviously—and typically ignored by literary theorists, this packaging also provides a component of a text's meaning.

Sometimes, when you write something down, your audience reads your words back from the same surface. This surface may be heavy and immobile, as when you laboriously inscribe a masonry facade or gravestone, paint signage on a building, or tag a railway embankment with spray-can graffiti. In these cases, the place gives meaning to the text, and the text gives meaning to the place.

Alternatively, the writing surface may be light and portable—papyrus, parchment, or paper. Notes, letters, newspapers, and books made from lightweight materials carry mobile messages—with their origins and destinations inflecting their meanings. We wouldn't be able to follow epistolary novels like *Pamela* if we didn't read letters with their movements in mind. A monumental inscription is "at" but a letter is "to" and "from."

With both static and mobile texts, the materials, details, and production qualities serve the purposes of writers semantically as well as physically. A handwritten letter on elegant, scented notepaper presents itself as a billet-doux, but a laser-printed sequence of paragraphs on a lawyer's letterhead presents itself as a billet-something-else. Furthermore, there may be an intangible but powerful aura derived from direct contact with the author's hand, or even with the press of a craft publisher like William Morris. A modern facsimile reprint, no matter how meticulously done, isn't the same as a Kelmscott Press original.

At some point in the mid-twentieth century, digital technology gradually began to disrupt this ancient game. Writers started to type text into computers, where it was stored and moved around electronically, in digital format—stripped of its traditional material underlays, to be re-embodied at some later point on the same display screen, on different, maybe distant screens, or in variously formatted and produced printouts. The words "input" and "output," previously applied to the raw materials and products of oil refineries and sewage treatment plants, became transitive verbs with text files as their objects.

Digital text began as a computer lab curiosity, but it swiftly took over everywhere. Over the last half-century, our culture has absorbed, and has been transformed by email, text messages, word processing, Web pages, and electronic publishing in its proliferating forms. Handwritten notes have become rarities, reserved for special occasions that require a particularly personal touch. By the fiftieth anniversary of Jack Kerouac's *On the Road,* of which the author reported to Neal Cassady that he had typed the "whole thing on strip of paper 120 foot long . . . just rolled it through typewriter and in fact no paragraphs . . . rolled it out on floor and it looks like a road," typewriters had disappeared.

Now, Amazon's introduction of the Kindle wireless reading device has dramatically rewritten the rules once again. A Kindle is a mobile digital device, about the size and weight of a paperback book. Through continuous connection with the Sprint's cellular data network, it enables one-minute downloads of books, magazines, and newspapers—any place, any time—for reading on a decent-sized, paperlike screen. It eliminates the need to go to a library, bookstore, newsstand, or even a WiFi hotspot with your laptop. It also makes all books look exactly the same—like small pages of black-and-white print in cheap plastic picture frames.

A few minute's use confirms that it is a typical first-generation product—a sorry little device with many technical limitations and design flaws, but maybe, as its business plan must anticipate, just good enough to open up a mass-market for some more capable successors. It takes the electronic book metaphor far too literally, providing a black leather notebooklike cover, and an "electronic paper" screen using E Ink technology. It is messy in appearance (no iPhone elegance, I'm afraid) and uncomfortable to hold. Most crucially, it makes the ill-advised design tradeoff of sacrificing interactivity and display quality for faux paper and longer battery life.

Thinking of the Kindle as a new kind of book is like thinking of the automobile as a horseless carriage, or radio frequency communication as wireless telegraphy. It assimilates a technological innovation that provides radically new capabilities to a familiar tradition, and so makes it understandable and marketable. But this obscures its more surprising, disruptive, longer-term potential. Just as automobiles soon lost their early buggylike styling and became streamlined sheet metal, so you can expect the Kindle to shed its leather cover as this potential becomes more obvious.

So you shouldn't let the absurdly high introductory price and first-generation infelicities of the Kindle fool you. (Remember; the first personal computers didn't look very promising, either, and the first laptop resembled a jumbo briefcase filled with bricks.) It is a genuine harbinger of a revolution in the embodiment and distribution of text—one that compares to the transition from scroll to codex, or even that from manuscript to printed page.

In combination with ubiquitous wireless connectivity and vast online text collections like those being developed by Google and Amazon, electronic reading devices will radically remake traditional relationships of text, materiality, place, and meaning. Where the ancient library of Alexandria sought to concentrate the world's literature in one place and to create a highly exclusive community of scholars around that unique center, these devices now demonstrate that every last line of it can be everywhere.

All that is text melts into air.

25

MAN OF STEEL

"Hey, I'm walkin' here!" That, of course, is the unforgettable line from *Midnight Cowboy*—Ratso Rizzo's affronted response to a New York cab that happened to cross his path. It was pretty much the reaction, too, of New Yorkers to Richard Serra's "Tilted Arc" when it was installed in front of a mediocre government office building in lower Manhattan's Federal Plaza in 1981. Serra's confrontational chunk of curved Cor-Ten got in their way to wherever, and it made them crazy.

The outraged Ratsos here were federal judges and bureaucrats, who successfully campaigned for its destruction. This took place in the small hours of the morning in 1989. It was a noisily contested but forward-looking move by the feds, long before the Taliban had demonstrated best practice in deaccessioning monuments at Bamiyan. All seems forgiven, though, at the triumphant Serra retrospective currently running at the Museum of Modern Art. The crowds are huge, the critics have raved, and the fat catalog costs $75.00 plus tax.

This is not surprising; Serra's cumulative achievement is undeniably magnificent, and it's fascinating to watch him hurl challenge after challenge at the received idea that works of sculpture are handcrafted things on pedestals. It began in the 1960s, when he started to hang rubber belts from hooks, and toss ladlefuls of molten lead to create layers of solidified splashes. The resulting works are formed not by the meticulous application of sculptor's tools, but by loosely controlled processes of materials responding to gravity. They are action paintings in space.

By the late sixties he had moved to his "Prop Pieces," constructed from simple slabs and rolls of lead. These are precariously balanced against each other, or against the walls. Here, it's a game of precisely managing force vectors. It's as if a poet had decided to illustrate a statics textbook. And because everything sags a bit under its own weight, the sheer mass of the gray, scarred, and blemished metal becomes silently threatening. You can see that there would be some serious damage if anything fell down.

In the seventies he turned to precision-rolled, flat sheets of steel, revealed at their edges to be—astonishingly—several inches thick. He arranged these in simple, tense configurations that sucked viewers in; it's minimalist sublime. "Delineator," on display at MOMA, consists simply of a large, black, rectangular sheet on the floor, that you're invited to walk on, together with a similar sheet, rotated ninety degrees, on the ceiling. The curators comment: "A dialogue is established between ceiling and floor, insistently affecting the viewer traveling through the environment." In other words, you're scared that it will squish you like a bug.

The real stars of the show, though, are the more recent, enormous, continuous, doubly curved pieces of sheet steel. Serra is cagey about exactly how these were produced, but it must have been through a digitally controlled factory rolling process done to precise mathematical specifications. "Intersection II," and "Torqued Ellipse IV," displayed in the Sculpture Garden, date from the 1990s. "Sequence," "Band," and "Torqued Torus Inversion," shown among the white walls of the second floor Contemporary Galleries, were made in 2006. They create sequences of dizzying, disorienting spatial experiences that can only be accessed by walking through them. The crowds line up for this, as for Disneyland rides.

The MOMA setting is crucial to their effect, and this tells us something about the relationships of art, space, and the experience economy. Looking back, it's obvious now. If the supporters of "Tilted Arc" had wanted pedestrians to value the spatial thrill it provided, rather than resent its intrusiveness, they should have put a fence around it and charged admission.

26

IT'S NOT EASY

The summer 2007 space opera *Sunshine* wasn't worth seeing, but Anthony Lane's review in the *New Yorker* was worth reading just for its opening lines: "Climate change is coming, and it's serious. None of the traditional folk remedies—switching to a Prius, recycling your eggshells, or taping the Bon Jovi set from the Live Earth concert—will avail you now."

As Lane had noticed, flaunting the emblems of environmental consciousness has become the secular equivalent of wearing a cross or a burka. It's a way of reassuring yourself of your virtue, and simultaneously, of advertising it to others. These symbols may represent real commitments and sacrifices, but they don't have to. Socially, it suffices that they are recognizable. And just as well: Al Gore has upped the pressure on all right-thinking citizens, but in the immortal words of Kermit the Frog, it's not easy being green.

One useful move is to insist, as the Bush administration has done to justify its opposition to Kyoto Protocol, that carbon emissions goals should be "aspirational." (My spell-checker, by the way, chokes on that unlovely neologism.) This is a wonderful idea, since it allows the public announcement of your firm dedication to virtue without the inconvenience of actually having to do anything about it. It's not hard to get agreement on goals that don't commit anyone to anything concrete, and this can be presented as a victory for hardheaded pragmatism—while critics are dismissed as naive utopians. As a way of taking the pressure off, this clearly has wide application. Any day now, I expect the pope to announce that celibacy is an aspirational goal for the priesthood.

Another way to pass for green is to purchase carbon credits. Nations, companies, and individuals can avail themselves of this handy option. Carbon trading schemes allow them to continue wasting energy, polluting, and warming the planet so long as they pay someone else to do something—such as planting trees—that partially counteracts their excesses. The rich don't have to act responsibly, so long as they can get the poor to do it for them.

As George Monbiot recently noted in the *Guardian*, this has the additional advantage of creating opportunities for economic innovation in the developing world. Entrepreneurs can, for example, make billions by building factories whose primary purpose is to produce greenhouse gases, so that carbon traders from rich countries will pay to clean them up.

Why not extend this sound economic principle to a universal system of asshole mitigation credits? This would be a win-win. It would work for upper-tax-bracket jackasses, who could continue, without guilt, to behave as badly as they have always felt entitled to. And for the economically disadvantaged, who need tough love, there would always be cash incentives they couldn't afford to forgo. As all readers of the *Wall Street Journal* editorial page know, the trouble with poor people is that they lack personal responsibility. They need punishments and rewards, and to be held accountable for their actions. This system would assure their good behavior—more effectively than preachers, jail, or cutting off their welfare payments.

Poor people are also the big problem with international pacts on carbon cutting, like Kyoto. Unfortunately, all those poor countries out there want to become rich countries. If they succeed, their energy consumption and carbon emissions levels will rise to those of the United States—which is terribly selfish of them. It's hard to argue publicly that they should know their place and stay as they are. It's costly to help them out with the finance and technology transfer that would enable them to create clean, efficient infrastructures, buildings, and industrial processes. So it's safest to use them as political cover. Argue that the rich countries really can't be expected to sign anything unless the poor countries first "bite the bullet" and curtail their irresponsible aspirations.

At an architectural scale, it is best to avoid the difficulty and expense of *actually* making projects energy-efficient and carbon-neutral. To show that you care, it is easier just to put some solar panels or wind turbines on conspicuous display, like the Golden Arches in front of a McDonald's. They don't really have to supply much of your building's energy needs, and that's fortunate, because they are expensive, and you will not be able to afford many of them. Think of them as talismans, providing magical cloaks of invisibility. You can be sure that nobody will look past them to check out the more questionable aspects of the rest of your project.

Be careful, though. The Greenies you want to impress tend to be sentimental nature lovers, and they will often object to solar and wind installations—particularly when these are big enough to make a worthwhile difference—because they seem like "industrial" intrusions into natural landscapes. In that case, just boast about your recycled water and fluorescent lightbulbs, and go with some grass on the roof.

27

IMAGINED WALL STREET

New York's *Wall Street Journal*—recently in the news itself as the quavering object of Rupert Murdoch's beady-eyed desire—has long been a joke. With its grim and old-fashioned typography, this cheerleader for red-blooded capitalism that couldn't make a profit has seemed a relic from another era. And its natural turf has inexorably been eroded by upstart competitors. If you wanted business news and analysis, then there was the much livelier *Economist*. If you wanted efficient delivery of market information, then you could go to *Bloomberg*. If you had a taste for ranting right wing editorializing and Neanderthal social attitudes, then *Fox News* and talk radio could supply all you wanted. The widespread, anguished bleating about its reduction to a vassal enterprise of the global Murdoch Empire has mostly been an expression of the old New York establishment's snobbery, provincialism, and injured pride.

Still, the gray, drab broadsheet had character, and it *was* a genuine part of the city. When Murdoch and his ruthless Australians transform it into a much more formidable competitor on the global stage, as they undoubtedly intend to do, it will be missed. Locally produced and circulated daily print may be dying, but it still plays a significant role in forming a sense of place. I wouldn't want to go without the *Boston Globe,* still tossed onto my doorstep every morning. It remains a thrill to grab a *New York Times,* or the more scandalous *Post* (with better headlines), from a newsstand in Grand Central Station. And it's still one of the delights of travel to find an unfamiliar local newspaper hanging on my hotel room door when I wake up—even if it's in Korean, and I can't read a word. Pick up a paper, and you feel that you're taking the pulse of the surrounding community.

Like nation states, modern cities are far too large for their inhabitants to have any chance of all knowing one another—violating a condition that Plato and Aristotle thought was crucial to community. Instead, to use Benedict Anderson's famous phrase, they are "imagined communities"—held together by common symbolic constructions in the minds of citizens. By circulating symbols and narratives, local newspapers have helped to produce and sustain these constructions. As times have changed, the *Wall Street Journal* has been a reassuring constant. It has continued to provide New Yorkers with imagined membership of the capital of capital, grounded on the iconic physical space of Wall Street, the Stock Exchange, and the towers of Lower Manhattan—even as much of the actual financial action has gradually diffused to other nodes in an increasingly extended network, the old street itself has became a tatty pedestrian mall, and the trading floor of the Stock Exchange has shrunk.

These days, though, local newspapers are undeniably in decline, and many of us now get much of our daily news from our personal selections of websites. For myself, wherever I happen to be in the world, I surf the online *New York Times,* the *Guardian* from London, *Le Monde* from Paris, the *Sydney Morning Herald,* and *Yahoo* from some indeterminate place. These sites keep us connected as never before, but they are all parasitic on print. Surely it's only a matter of time before the parasite kills the host.

In response to the steady erosion of the urban role of print, several of New York's major news organizations have recently made different bets on the future—mostly with expensive architecture to match. The *Wall Street Journal* has gone with Murdoch, wherever that may lead. *Bloomberg* has built a slick, twenty-first-century, online information processing hub. The Hearst Corporation has constructed a triangulated Norman Foster tower over the uncompleted 1927 Hearst building on 57th Street. The *New York Times* has just moved into a monumental Renzo Piano tower in Midtown, with a facade treatment recalling columns of classified ads and a traditional newsroom done in corporate-modern by Gensler.

It will be interesting to see how these bold (maybe desperate) moves pay off. Someone will get to form the imagined New York of the coming decades, but my guess is that it will not be any of these.

28

THE EAGLE FLIES

That Range-Rover-sized aluminum eagle atop the American Embassy in Grosvenor Square—like a mutant in a monster movie—has always seemed ready to pick up the whole thing and fly away with it. Maybe it has been telling us something. According to recent media reports, the embassy is now selling up and moving to the safety of the suburbs; an urban setting doesn't allow a sufficiently secure perimeter, and anyway, there's too much glass.

This big-box, one-stop diplomatic shop resulted from a competition won by Eero Saarinen in the 1950s. Saarinen seemed to have an inside track on embassy work in those days, and he produced several major projects—none of which has fared well.

His ambitious scheme for Helsinki went unexecuted, apparently because he lost his patron at the State Department in a political reshuffle. In Oslo, however, he was commissioned to build on a prominent site opposite the royal palace, where he responded with an updated Renaissance palazzo, complete with inner court, soberly clad with granite-colored precast panels. This broke with the tradition of embassies that looked like big, fancy villas in gardens; it was explicitly urban; and it made some contextualizing gestures—coming right up to the street, rising to the height of the surrounding buildings, and completing the street wall. But times have changed. The Embassy website now announces that the Saarinen building "fails to meet current security standards." After much NIMBY-dogged negotiation, U,S, officials have purchased a property on the outskirts of the city, where they plan to construct a fortress in the forest.

The site for the new embassy in London, with its grand setting on a Georgian square, must have seemed invitingly palazzo-ready. Saarinen produced a bilaterally symmetrical scheme that held the street with an enormous rectangular facade, and provided an imposing entrance in the middle. Vertically, there was a clear classical subdivision into basement, piano nobile, and attic zones. The basement level had a vestigial loggia, and was glazed rather than rusticated, which turned out to be a problem when Vietnam-era protestors began throwing rocks at it. The piano nobile segment rose in four floors to accommodate hundreds of State Department bureaucrats, and ultimately degenerated into a tired and dreary office warren. The cladding system carefully imitated the proportions and rhythms of Georgian windows—a contextualist gesture that infuriated modernist critics who wanted to see a straightforward structural frame. When it was all done, Saarinen ruefully reflected: "In my own mind, the building is much better than the English think—but not quite as good as I wished it to be."

The story of the great Renaissance villas and palaces can be read as one of shedding the fortifications of the castle—enabling villas to embrace the countryside, and palaces to engage the streets. For a brief, optimistic, postwar moment—before Vietnam, Beirut, Baghdad, and the car bombers—the American Embassy projects of Saarinen and other mid-century modernists did the same. It would be a mistake to romanticize the Cold War cultural politics of which they were so clearly a part, and the palazzo-inspired embassies aren't among Saarinen's best buildings, but they did represent something very attractive: an America that celebrated openness, and wanted to be closely, sensitively, and respectfully engaged with the cities of its allies.

Today, it's back to Crusaders in the Krak des Chevaliers.

29

ARCHITECTURAL ASSASSINATION

Some things—polyester pants, invading Iraq, paying O. J. Simpson to write his memoirs—belong in the Bad Ideas Hall of Fame. Recently, Boston's mayor, Thomas Menino, has introduced a hot new prospect for induction. His heavily hyped Bad Idea is to demolish Boston City Hall, sell the historic downtown site to developers, and with the proceeds build a new one that's more to his liking on the far fringes of the central business district. It's plan for a hit that Tony Soprano—hatching them in the Club Bada-Bing—might have admired.

Even if you have never visited Beantown, you probably know its City Hall. An early project of the distinguished Boston firm Kallmann/McKinnell, it was the winner of a major architectural competition in the 1960s. This was the time of macho-monumental cast-in-place concrete with obligatory allusions to late Corb. Within that idiom, it was ambitious in its conception, brilliant in its execution, and vividly evocative of its particular cultural moment. It immediately entered the modernist canon.

Of course, this uncompromising icon has always had plenty of local detractors—Boston being a place where bland brick boxes with desultory neo-Georgian detailing meet widespread approval because they are thought to fit in. Furthermore, its interior spaces have long been in need of renovation to meet twenty-first-century requirements, and many of them have deteriorated into drab gloominess. So it has become an inviting target for demagogues pursuing various agendas. If you are a developer looking for a lucrative payday, an aging politician looking for a legacy, or a tabloid columnist looking to stick it to pointy-headed intellectuals and out-of-touch architectural elitists, you can quickly silence any debate by stringing together a few tendentious adjectives like "monstrous," "brutal," and "dank." This is the culture-wars equivalent of Carl Rove's political campaigning (the Swift-boating of John Kerry, say), and if you can get some of the negatives to stick, it's equally effective.

But there's a highly questionable cultural assumption behind the mayor's attempt to play the antimodernist card. It's that functions and meanings can readily be decanted from one building to another. Sure, you can take down the name above the door and move it someplace else. And you can shift people, organizational units, and their activities. You can bring in trucks to move the files and office furniture. But the culture of a building is a fragile web that doesn't easily survive transplanting. Associations and memories tend to stick to the place where they were formed. And meaning that derives from a historic, genuinely central location in a city isn't transferable to the outskirts.

It's always possible, of course, that the reconstituted functional patterns and meanings of a new building will be preferable to those left behind in the old. But I wouldn't count on it here. It's worth remembering that Winston Churchill's famous remark about making buildings, and then our buildings making us, was a response to a proposal to demolish and rebuild the House of Commons. He wouldn't have it. In this case, his cranky conservatism was right.

Architects clearly have a particular responsibility to provide a broader historical and urbanistic perspective than political advantage seekers and real estate opportunists, to emphasize that architectural value isn't just a matter of fleeting current taste, and to speak out vigorously against threats of architectural assassination. But that's not enough; they must also demonstrate graceful and compelling ways to accommodate new programs and systems within the aging monuments of modernism, and stand ready to provide convincing alternatives to the simplistic demolish-and-redevelop proposals that these will undoubtedly face with increasing frequency.

It's urgent, since the timing of the campaign to trash City Hall couldn't be better. Owing to the usual swings of fashion, the relics of mid-century modernism are currently at their most vulnerable. The passions and debates that motivated them are no longer current in the schools and journals. The advocates of opposing architectural directions have had their say. The revivalist polemics have not yet appeared. This is precisely the sort of juncture at which communities need to take the greatest care with their architectural patrimony. It is when value is hardest to recognize, and when great losses are most likely.

In the past, Bostonians have suffered schemes that, it can only be said, seemed like good ideas at the time—as when their beloved Red Sox sold Babe Ruth to the New York Yankees. Let's hope that they will have the foresight and wisdom to reject this one. Like banishment of the Babe, destruction of City Hall would leave an aching civic void.

30

URBAN PLASTINATION

If you search on "mother and child," it comes up in Google Images. But it isn't a nativity scene. Damien Hirst's "Mother and Child, Divided" makes art out of dead meat. It inverts the myth of Galatea, in which Aphrodite transformed Pygmalion's ivory sculpture into living flesh.

Hirst's cheeky exercise in Duchamp-inspired appropriation, which was exhibited at the Venice Biennale in 1993, consists of a bisected cow alongside a similarly sliced calf. The half-carcasses are preserved in facing tanks of formaldehyde. You can promenade past the entrails as if strolling down Fifth Avenue to inspect the Christmas windows.

If these animals were still living out their humble lives they would be nothing more than livestock or zoo specimens—not art on the hoof. If you found them in a butcher's window they would just be steak and veal. If they were stuffed and mounted on the wall they would be uninteresting examples of taxidermy. If you saw them in the Museum of Natural History you wouldn't give them a second look. But when you encounter them in a gallery among other works, you know that they are high-priced offerings in the art market. Their flesh has become far more valuable as representation of former life than it ever was as the real thing.

30

Hirst is big in New York this holiday season. Although hedge funds are going belly-up everywhere, a hedge fund fortune has financed the meticulous restoration of his famous shark-in-a-box piece "The Physical Impossibility of Death in the Mind of Someone Living," and it is pulling visitors into the Metropolitan Museum of Art. In the Lever House lobby gallery, his bumper Christmas show demonstrates the ongoing diversification of his cadaver art palette. Arranged on a Manhattan-like grid, he gives us thirty sheep in vitro, a shark, two frozen sides of beef, three hundred sausages, and a pair of doves.

He doesn't end with a dead partridge in a pear tree, but the show does put you in the mood for the nearby Barney's holiday windows on the theme "Twelve Green Days of Christmas," featuring Rudolph the Recycling Reindeer. Disappointingly, it turns out that Barney's isn't as edgy as it likes to suggest, and Rudolph isn't actually a recycled reindeer carcass.

Formaldehyde is a bit smelly, and it confers a retro look, which probably suits Hirst's artistic purposes. A more up-to-date preservation technique is plastination, in which all those messy fats and fluids in biological specimens are replaced by firm, dry, odorless polymer. This cleans everything up nicely. It was developed by Gunther von Hagens, a Barnum-like figure in a fedora who creates crowd-pleasing tableaux out of human corpses that have been run through the process, carefully sashimied to reveal their internal organs, and arranged in lifelike poses. His Body Worlds show is currently a hit in Charlotte, San Jose, and Saint Louis, but surprisingly, it hasn't yet joined Madame Tussaud's on 42nd Street.

Like figures in snapshots, or the mannequins representing old Venice, Vienna, Paris, and Copenhagen in Lord & Taylor's holiday windows, von Hagens's plastinated cadavers eternally enact moments from the past. They have no futures. That man hunched over a chessboard, with his cranium split open to show his brain, will never make his move. That pregnant woman, with her womb cut away to reveal the fetus, will never give birth.

Architectural preservationists are in much the same business as Hirst and von Hagens, but the tools of their trade are different. Buildings don't rot as quickly as corpses, so they don't require the application of formaldehyde or polymer. As Duchamp would have recognized, the essential thing here is a speech act—a declaration, by someone with sufficient clout, that a place formerly containing the messiness of ongoing life has now become an untouchable, overvalued representation of what it once was. Consequently, its narrative is truncated. So the house where Robert Louis Stevenson died in the tropical rainforest of Vailima is meticulously kept as a snapshot of that instant, and the house where Leon Trotsky was murdered in Coyoacán has not changed in nearly seventy years. You can still see his paper-strewn desk and wire-rimmed glasses as he left them.

The trouble is that cities are not museums or Christmas windows. Preserving the lifeless carcasses of buildings provides spectacle, and it attracts tourists, but it cannot produce vital urban areas. And, as you can see vividly in the historic centers of Venice and Florence these days, the effects compound insidiously. First, the increasing difficulty of daily life in an area that cannot adapt to evolving needs drives out the traditional inhabitants. Next, the small food stores and other enterprises that served them shut down and are replaced by tourist boutiques. Furthermore, the number of children diminishes, so the neighborhood schools close, and this discourages families from moving in. Finally, a new population of affluent visitors, weekend residents, and expatriates replaces what was there before and completes the process of urban plastination.

As a person of faith, I like to ask myself, "What would Aphrodite do?" I think she would recognize that the real life of these cities is more important than its plastinated remains—no matter how evocative and culturally significant these may be—and get to work on bringing it back. She would respect the past, but accept the importance of sensitively managed growth and change. She would insist that the stories of these great places cannot remain arrested at canonical points in the past, but must—like that of Galatea—continue.

31

CIVIC IMMUNOLOGY

Christmas, 2007. A bitter *New Yorker* cover shows Santa in a military helicopter with two machine-gun-toting guards—Blackwater style—hanging off the sides.

It is now six years since 9/11, five since President George W. Bush rolled out his fraudulent case for invading Iraq, and four since he stood on the deck of the USS *Abraham Lincoln* to announce, "Mission accomplished." In Sydney a few months ago, he chortled to Australia's deputy prime minister—who was soon to be swept out of office in an electoral landslide—"We're kicking ass." It is time for an accounting.

The principal measurable accomplishments of Dubya's trillion-dollar military adventure have been: to destroy Iraq's infrastructure and institutions; to kill and maim hundreds of thousands of people; and to make daily life even more miserable and dangerous than it was under the vile Saddam Hussein. When they are not on armed missions, the invaders remain huddled within their heavily fortified Green Zone. The longer the occupation drags on, the higher the body count—not that anyone bothers to keep track of the Iraqi dead. They are just nameless, numberless collateral damage.

Surprisingly, the Iraqis are not grateful. So former cheerleaders for the bombing, invasion, and occupation are now preparing for the inevitable face-saving exit by complaining that those impossible Arabs, who neglected to greet their conquerors with flowers, just don't deserve us.

But this raises the question of where the chastened citizens of the rapidly shrinking coalition of the willing might withdraw *to*. The discomfiting answer is that there are no safe havens. There is no such thing as impregnable homeland security. It is no use hopefully repeating, "Fight them over there so we won't have to fight them here." The global ubiquity of transportation and telecommunication networks, on which modern economies, cities, and nations depend, creates opportunities for just about anyone to reach out and harm us anywhere. These networks provide what Mike Davis has called the "poor man's air force."

This development is certainly unwelcome, but hardly surprising. Criminals have always responded to new urban conditions, infrastructures, and modes of connection with innovative schemes for taking advantage of them. As soon as there were camel trains connecting trading cities there were bandits attacking them. Renaissance cities provided plentiful opportunities for Montague and Capulet thuggery in alleys with swords. Mercantile cities and their sailing-ship networks had to contend with pirates. Intercity coach networks spawned highwaymen. Early industrial cities, with their crowded streets, bred pickpockets and muggers. More advanced industrialization, bringing inexpensive automobiles and firearms, created the conditions for stickups and getaways, and for college campus shooting sprees.

These days, our vehicle-choked cities, with parking spaces and vehicle access at just about every building, make us vulnerable to car and truck bombing. (The rings of Jersey barriers that were hastily strung around buildings after 9/11, and mostly still remain, are vivid reminders of this.) Our global air networks make us prey to hijackers. Our postal networks can carry lethal packages. Our water supply and air-conditioning networks can precisely deliver toxins and biological agents to building inhabitants. Our extended oil and natural gas supply lines are not only subject to disruption, but can also erupt in deadly explosions. Our cell phone networks provide bombers with convenient remote detonation capability. Our computer networks allow not only our personal computers, but also crucial servers and control systems, to be hacked—or to be threatened with hacking by blackmailers. The arts of hijacking, car bombing, suicide bombing, letter bombing, and cybercrime are thriving. Their practitioners are numerous, inventive, and resourceful.

New urban conditions create not only new means and opportunities for criminals, but also new motives. Global telecommunications networks, flows of people, and enterprises now bring incompatible cultures and beliefs that would once have been safely separated into inescapable confrontation. And they pitilessly expose staggering differences between the lives of the wealthy few and the struggling many. You don't have to be a sympathizer with criminals or blamer of victims to recognize that these fault lines will reliably generate alienation, despair, envy, vengefulness, rage, and all the other dangerous emotions that novelists tirelessly explore. (Incidentally, from the recent crop, I recommend John Updike's *The Terrorist* and Richard Flanagan's *The Unknown Terrorist.*) There will always be some who are driven by these emotions to attack lives and property. There will always be ideologies—from that of Harry Lime to that of violent jihad—to assure them that they are justified. And there will always be startup enterprises to replace any—the one led by Osama bin Laden, say—that might eventually be eliminated.

Some of the nastiest of today's new-wave criminals (those who announce that they want to kill anyone who doesn't share their beliefs) have emerged from the psychopathic fringes of the Islamic world, but they have never been confined to any particular national, ethnic, or religious group. So, to construct the comforting illusion of a coherent enemy that can readily be identified and defeated in a "war on terror," it is necessary to avoid concrete specifics ("terror," conveniently, does not refer to anyone in particular) while denying any such diversity. It is necessary, for example, to suppress memories of: the Oklahoma City bomber with his rented Ryder truck and industrial chemicals; the Unabomber's exploitation of the U.S. postal network; Aum Shinrikyo's sarin nerve gas attack on the Tokyo subway network; the Provisional IRA's Bloody Friday in Belfast; the Tamil Tigers' signature roadside bombings in Sri Lanka; the ETA's Hipercor department store bombing in Barcelona; the Mafia's car-bombing of the Uffizi in Florence; the Birmingham, Alabama, abortion clinic bombing; the mysterious introduction of anthrax spores into the air circulation systems of buildings in Washington; and the 2007 cyber attacks on Estonia's computer infrastructure. And it is necessary to forget that many terrorists turn out to be "home grown."

What follows from this amnesia is repeated assurance that a vaguely and elastically specified "they" (but, no doubt, buddies of Saddam) "hate us," and want to destroy "our way of life." The vagueness of this terminology is a telltale sign. These formulations are semantic swindles—verbal constructions that, as George Orwell observed in "Politics and the English Language," "not only do not point to any discoverable object, but are hardly ever expected to do so by the reader." This sort of language is used by ideologists and propagandists in defense of the indefensible, when it is necessary to name things without raising embarrassing questions about what, precisely, is intended. It is employed here slyly to suggest that destroying Baghdad, and maybe Tehran as well, will protect American and European cities from future attack by eliminating the bad guys once and for all. Fear, racism, and cultural chauvinism reliably do the rest.

But there is an alternative to this futile and destructive strategy of dividing the world into green zones for "us" and war zones for "them." It is to realistically confront the fact that the cities of the twenty-first century are so densely and inextricably interconnected by movement systems, interchanges of population, and communication networks as to constitute an indivisible global system, and that these new criminal threats arise internally to it. There are no clear boundaries between us and them, no places to draw secure perimeters.

So, instead of attempting to re-create the walled condition of ancient times, as illustrated by modern Baghdad's Green Zone prototype, we should work on developing ubiquitous, adaptive immune systems for our cities. These, like our bodily immune systems, should be capable of responding to threats and attacks wherever these may emerge. The Internet provides a model for this. Its essential elements are globally distributed rather than concentrated in one place, and highly redundant rather than unique. It has sufficient adaptive intelligence to continue functioning, through automatic utilization of its remaining capability, whenever part of it is damaged or destroyed. And it has an increasingly sophisticated, continually evolving, dispersed system of firewalls and filters that limit the propagation of damaging agents.

The urban systems and patterns that we have inherited from the industrial era have responded to the imperatives of specialization, economies of scale, and predigital technologies, so they generally lack these properties. Organizations have concentrated their employees in extremely vulnerable towers, like those that were attacked on 9/11, but they should now consider dispersed systems of smaller facilities held together by sophisticated networking. Transportation systems have been built around a few major hubs and high-capacity links, but they should now develop more distributed and redundant structures. (Airline networks are already restructuring along these lines.) Electrical grids have made use of small numbers of large power plants, but they should now treat buildings as small-scale electrical producers—employing solar, wind, and microgeneration capabilities—as well as consumers, so that cities become distributed virtual power plants.

These strategies all illustrate one general principle. When the advantages of large-scale concentration of resources and activities are great, and the associated risks seem small, it makes sense for cities to develop around a few large facilities interconnected by a few high-capacity links. But, when advances in transportation and telecommunication simultaneously reduce the advantages of concentration and increase its risk, while increasing the feasibility of dispersion, cities should begin to evolve finer-grained, mixed-use, redundantly interconnected structures. This reduces their vulnerability not only to attacks, but also to system failures, accidents, and natural disasters. The necessary adaptation will take time and resources, but it is certainly technologically feasible, and it is preferable to pouring those resources into futile quagmire wars.

Beyond this, there is a further urban lesson to be learned from the Internet. Just as the Internet recognizes that threats cannot be localized, takes the existence of viruses and spam (which may originate anywhere in the world) as a fact of life, and employs filters and firewalls everywhere to protect computers and subnetworks from them, so the designers and managers of cities should assume the general existence of easily concealed and propagated explosives, toxins, and weapons. In response, they should make use of electronic detection technologies to create similar systems of local barriers around buildings and neighborhoods. We already see the crude and intrusive beginnings of this at airport security checkpoints, in the metal detectors at the entrances to public buildings, and in electronic mail and cargo monitoring systems.

It should be a technology development priority to increase the effectiveness of sensing and detection technologies, and to drive down their costs, so that they can be deployed ubiquitously, not just at high-value locations. But they will not work in practice if their burden on everyday life is too high. So it will also be necessary to increase their social acceptability through convenient and graceful architectural integration and through insistence upon implementations and operating policies that provide strong protection of individual dignity and privacy—obviously not primary considerations, so far, in the wretched airport security systems we have all been subjected to since 9/11.

A closely related, complementary strategy is expansion of electronic identification and authentication of pedestrians, vehicles, and packages. Currently, this takes the forms of card-key access control systems in buildings, transponder systems for controlling car access to parking and for automatically charging tolls, and RFID tagging of products and packages. The technology is available to make electronic access control fine-grained, ubiquitous, and extremely sophisticated. A far greater challenge will be to develop broadly acceptable policy frameworks for its use—frameworks that appropriately safeguard individual privacy, and that provide vigorous protection against electronically implemented discrimination and victimization.

Reducing the vulnerability of urban populations in these ways should reduce the fear of unexpected violence and reduce the ability of demagogues to appeal to that fear. (How else, but in an atmosphere of continually stoked fear, could politicians elected by decent people get away undermining habeas corpus, freedom to speak and assemble, and other cherished rights?) But this will not, of course, eliminate crime. Within a framework of dispersed functionality, redundant networks, and ubiquitous electronic sensing, filtering, and identification, cities will still need to respond to the entrepreneurial innovation of their criminals—as they have done at least since Caesar Augustus created squads of *Vigiles Urbani* to watch out for burglars (as well as fires and runaway slaves) in Rome—by continually evolving their safety, police, and criminal justice systems.

But innovative response to network-era crime should not mean heavily armed security contractors running around in Humvees, unaccountable electronic surveillance, rendition and torture, and military prisons beyond the reach of the law. On the contrary, it will be vital to resist panic and scrupulously protect civil liberties while developing and executing urban defense strategies—not only because this is the civilized thing in itself, but also because it confers legitimacy and establishes the citizen trust in governments and their agencies that is crucial to long-term success in intelligence gathering, police work, and criminal prosecution. It is particularly difficult to imagine public acceptance of electronic sensing, identification and authentication, and access control systems without strong assurance that these will not be misused and abused. Sadly, through their cynical fear mongering, their economy with the truth, and their treatment of legal protections as dispensable luxuries, 9/11-era political leaders like George Bush, Tony Blair, and the bit-players in their entourages have severely damaged that essential trust.

31

In the ruins of the War on Terror, there is a lot of repair work to do. Rebuilding squandered trust will be a difficult but crucial challenge for the next generation of leaders. If they have even modest success, this will do far more for the safety of our globally interconnected cities than the endless escalation of demands for draconian legal "tools," the branding of opponents as traitors from within, and the repetition of bombastic announcements that we will never surrender.

The ideologues who dragged us into the Iraq war will, of course, continue to suggest that all this is the counsel of fuzzyheaded sissies—alluding, when all else fails, to mushroom clouds over Manhattan. But Spain's recent apprehension, prosecution, and conviction of twenty-one perpetrators of the 2004 Madrid commuter train bombings has provided evidence that they are wrong. The police work was resourceful and meticulous. The trial was conducted openly, with creditable and convincing fairness, and it effectively teased out the complex story of the religious fanatics, former drug traffickers, small-time local crooks, and international terrorists who put the deadly scheme together. By responding in a firm but carefully measured way to a terrible crime, Spain has rekindled hope for open, democratic, and creative cities in the twenty-first century.

Meanwhile, a letter to Santa in his chopper: I've been good, so I suppose I have nothing to fear, but I'm not happy about being on your watch list. Anyway, you'll never get that bag through airport security.

32

WORLD'S GREATEST ARCHITECT

I'd love to know how God ran his office in the beginning. Somehow, he got an amazing amount done. Even a Dubai developer might think that the intelligent design and construction of everything there is, in just six days, was too much of a miracle to ask for.

He did have some advantages, of course. For one thing, it was about 6,000 years ago. (He's even older than Phillip Johnson.) There were no contractors yet—certainly none with track records, so there was no bidding process. And omniscience meant that he didn't have to worry about errors and omissions. So he just took on all the liability himself, and went design-build—which enabled him to bring the project in on time and on budget. It's unfortunate, though, that the water had to be value-engineered out of so much of the Middle East. That was short-sighted, and it's still causing operational and maintenance problems.

On the first day, as his assistants later recounted, he switched on the lights. Well, it was a start.

On the second day he created the Firmament, the world's biggest roof structure—even larger than the Millennium Dome. Then he began to wonder what to do with the space underneath. The thing wouldn't work, he realized, unless he had some hot-ticket attractions lined up. It could just sit there, vacant, for years.

On the third day he had a brilliant idea. He invented waterfront property, which is what you get when you let the waters under the heaven be gathered unto one place, and let the dry land appear. He called the development Earth, and he saw that it was good. The scientific establishment will try to tell you that the Earth's coastlines, with all their beautiful intricacies, resulted from natural processes. But could structures that are so complex, and so essential for the successful functioning of the real estate industry, have arisen through blind chance? I think not.

He also put in the landscaping—early, so that it would mature in time for the opening. The newly bulldozed landfill brought forth grass, the herb yielding seed, and the fruit tree yielding fruit. And the site supervisor saw to it that it was good.

On the fourth day he created the sun, the moon, and the stars. This wasn't strictly necessary, but he was after the Bilbao effect. He wanted some wow. When the zodiac lit up at night, he saw that it was worth every penny.

On the fifth day he discovered CAD monkeys. He hired dozens of them, and put them to work in a back room. He blessed them, saying, be productive and multiply drawings. He hadn't a clue how they did it, but they soon brought forth abundantly the moving creatures that hath life, the fowl that fly above the earth, the great whales, cattle, creeping things, and every living creature. This includes Paris Hilton—which proves that Darwin was wrong. How could a process of "survival of the fittest" have produced something so completely and utterly useless? Only a designer could do that.

On the sixth day, he got into blobs. He turned a 3-D scanner on himself to create a parametric NURBS model in his image, after his likeness. It had two structural supports, two horizontal extensions, and a sort of spherical thing with six openings on top. He assigned it the file name Adam, and made a CAD/CAM prototype. Then he adjusted a few variables, substituted a couple of parts, and cloned Eve. The model was mass-customizable; it could generate millions of variants, all of them slightly different. He saw every thing that he had made, and, behold, he was in the magazines.

On the seventh day he got a certificate of occupancy, then took a break. I understand that there was still quite a punch list to work through, though. Nobody's perfect.

Following this early success, he brought in partners and restructured as G.O.D Associates LLC, a multidisciplinary, full-service firm—a bit like Arups. GOD competed with SOM and HOK for the big international jobs. Enoch headed up the urban design division. Lamech was into tensile structures and metal fabrication. Noah specialized in marina developments and floating resorts. After a while, Cain went out on his own. Lord God (as he had become) still had his name on the door as the senior design partner, but the truth was that he now spent most of his time doing marketing and pontificating on television. That's why scholars of intelligent design are often hesitant to credit God, himself, as the actual designer of all things bright and beautiful, all creatures great and small. Most of them weren't signature projects—just bread-and-butter office jobs.

Not surprisingly, then, many of GOD's projects haven't stood the test of time. Eden didn't look bad in the published pictures, but it turned out to be a sterile and boring place to live—like Brasilia, Canberra, and Milton Keynes. Adam and Eve, the original power couple, voted with their feet—like Posh and Becks heading for California. They met a persuasive Apple salesman, got a figleaf-top, Googled some brochures, and were out of there.

God's biggest limitation was his authoritarian, top-down approach. He was a real Old Testament character—beard and all. He'd just dream something up and go, like, "Let there be whatever." He had never heard of Jane Jacobs, and he had no idea that the most complex, diverse, and interesting cities emerge, gradually over many years, from countless incremental interventions and adjustments. It's a bottom-up process, without a master plan. One thing just leads to another, and the most amazing results evolve in completely unexpected ways.

EPILOGUE: WRITING AND THE WEB

It seems that Francis Bacon wrote his *Essays* in his spare time. Even assuming that he wasn't scribbling Shakespeare on the side, there couldn't have been much of it. Between his precocious years at Trinity College, Cambridge, and his sensational fall from public life a quarter century later (after which he had the leisure to pursue his more systematic philosophical works), he was admitted to Gray's Inn, practiced as a lawyer, spent several years in Paris with the ambassador to France, urged the execution of Mary Queen of Scots, served successively as member of Parliament, solicitor general, attorney general, lord keeper, and lord chancellor, struggled with debt, pursued a wealthy widow, married a fourteen year old, and scandalized his mother by taking numerous young men as coach and bed companions.

Not surprisingly then, the individual essays are brief and crisp. They read as the products of reflective moments framed by a busy life. They are self-contained; their topics are as diverse as could be; and there is no discernible logic to the sequence in which they appear. But their cumulative effect—like that of a collection of random snapshots of some event—is to construct from details a larger picture of Elizabethan culture, politics, and conditions of daily existence. Furthermore, their ingredients and organizational patterns reveal the knowledge circulation practices of the day. Clearly they are formed by the Scholastic system of textual production—of reading, annotating, copying out fragments to notebooks, recombining, and adding commentary and argument—but they also find ways to challenge and subvert it.

Generations of readers have praised Bacon's objectivity, the lawyerly clarity of his arguments, and the forthright, symmetrical elegance of his prose—his advice, for example, on building: "Houses are built to live in, and not to look on; therefore let use be preferred before uniformity." Today, though, we may find ourselves more interested in his insistent interjection of qualifications and exceptions that highlight exceptions to general rules, his delight in paradox and contradiction, his skeptical asides, his sly efforts to undermine what he just said, and his unexpectedly broken rhythms. We notice that his sentence opposing functionality to beauty doesn't stop decisively where we might expect, but skids into " except where both may be had." Then he reminds us that beauty sometimes comes cheap—sort of; the enchanted palaces of poets are built with small cost.

Looking back, it seems to me that the essays collected here are best read as a modest remake of Bacon—with, of course, some degrees of separation from him. (The *Essays*, like *Breathless* and *Invasion of the Body Snatchers*, have assumed the role of grounding classic that invites a remake by every generation.) They were written between 2004 and 2007, and mostly appeared as monthly columns in the *Royal Institute of British Architects Journal* and the London weekly *Building Design*. The moments for them were found not only at my desk, but also on trains and airplanes, in departure lounges, hotels, and cafés scattered throughout the world, occasionally on beaches and park benches, and a couple of times with a drip in my arm in Massachusetts General Hospital. They would not have been possible without a wireless laptop computer that provided constant, mobile connectivity to the vast resources of the Internet and the World Wide Web, and they enabled immediate transmission to my editors and publishers from anywhere I happened to be. They are not the work of a scholar in a study with a mug of cocoa and cozy bookshelves, but of a professionally engaged, electronically connected nomad worrying about catching the next flight. If I wanted a warm drink I grabbed it from Starbuck's, and if I needed a book, I ordered it from Amazon.com and then packed it in my carry-on bag.

The system of knowledge circulation and textual production that the Web supports today, and from which these essays therefore derive, is usually hailed as an unprecedented phenomenon of revolutionary importance. In one sense, that's obviously true. But it can equally well be understood as supersized Scholasticism—highly automated, operating at vastly higher clock speed and bandwidth, but accreting, cross-linking, recombining, and classifying texts in much the same self-referential way. And it suffers from similar limitations—often much magnified. Hand copying to notebooks has become cut-and-paste. The Google index, with its keyword-derived categories and subcategories, is a clunking Aristotelian construction that relentlessly imposes itself upon everything and allows no escape. Blogs deposit layer upon layer of commentary and disputation on every conceivable topic, clogging the channels with enormous quantities of dispiriting verbal sludge. A typical Wikipedia entry is a multiauthored sequence of flat-footed, ambiguously reliable declarative sentences—maybe presenting to the search engines a useful consensus view on something of interest, but systematically purged of subtlety, freshness, and personal voice. Inescapably, this book is a product of the neo-scholastic global culture of the mid-zerozeroes, but it simultaneously attempts to be critical of it, and to pay attention to some of the more important ironies and fault lines.

In fragmented fashion, it mirrors its moment. In the tale of Y2K cities, you could say that the middle of the 00 decade—decidedly digital in its culture as it approached 10—was the best of times, it was the worst of times. Since events move fast while design and construction projects progress slowly, the rhythms of architectural and urban response are always syncopations of wider historical narratives, but I suspect we will look back upon this as a pivotal moment in urban history. It was the age of intellectual and economic liberation through global interconnectivity, and of the discovery by violent criminals that they could exploit worldwide transportation and telecommunication networks for their own miserable purposes. It was the epoch of instantly available knowledge, and of the construction of electronic police states. It was a springtime of new science and technology and a winter of stubborn ignorance and bigotry. It was the season of suicide bombers, of the disastrous war in Iraq, and of the shame of Guantánamo Bay.

INDEX